PENGUIN ANANDA

DHRUVA

Gauranga Darshan Das, a disciple of His Holiness Radhanath Swami, is an educator, TEDx speaker and a spiritual author of over thirty-two books. He holds a master's degree from the Indian Institute of Science, Bangalore. He is a resident of the ISKCON Govardhan Ecovillage (GEV) and serves as the dean of the Bhaktivedanta Vidyapitha. He is also a member of the ISKCON Board of Examinations and GEV Administrative Council.

He regularly delivers online and residential discourses for children and adults in various forums, including temples, ashrams, schools, colleges, corporate events and platforms such as TEDx, Defence Research and Development Organization (DRDO), Rotary Club, *Hindustan Times*, etc. He is a regular speaker on Hare Krsna TV. He has conducted over forty-five online courses (www.vidyapitha.in) and over 7500 hours of lectures. He travels to various places in India, Australia, United States, etc. to teach and inspire spiritual seekers.

Some of his literary contributions include the *Subodhini* series of study guides, the *Pravaha* series of storybooks, self-enrichment books like *Disapproved but Not Disowned*, children's book series like *Bhagavatam Tales* and *Gita Wisdom Tales*, and shloka compilations like the *Ratnamala* series. He runs a monthly ezine called Bhagavata Pradipika whilst penning thought-inspiring articles for international and Indian *Back to Godhead* magazines.

Find more about him on www.gaurangadarshan.com

Celebrating 35 Years of
Penguin Random House India

ADVANCE PRAISE FOR THE BOOK

'Taking the time to sit with this book *Dhruva* may require you to step back from the tyranny of the one thousand urgent things that demands your immediate attention. But it's definitely worth it—many times over! In *Dhruva,* you will find wisdom that breathes or is alive with potency handed down and preserved by the saints of the past, who are known as true well-wishers of humanity. When you step forward, you will get something, but when you step backwards and discover the wealth of the wisdom of Prince Dhruva, you may get everything. After all, Dhruva's material as well as spiritual attainments are still unprecedented in the history of mankind. Gauranga Darshan's *Dhruva* is certainly a book that needs to be read with the mind of a treasure hunter'—His Holiness Sacinandana Swami, monk, author and teacher

'Surpassing simplistic notions of success, the author weaves a compelling tapestry of timeless wisdom and contemporary insight. Ambitions, achievements and relationships, all reach their genuine, heartfelt fulfilment in this gentle yet crystal-clear guidebook for the good life—satisfaction both outer and inner'—His Holiness Devamrita Swami, author, monk and educator

'In the service of Krishna these days, one of the most challenging obstacles is relationships of all kinds. They are what fuel most of our motivations, as well as sometimes becom[e] the source of our greatest frustrations. It is no wonder, perhaps, that Gauranga Darshan's book has been written at a time when we must all look towards our own hearts, and the relationships within.

Dhruva is an excellent book to get started on that journey. The compilation of the book, blending the timeless wisdom of the Bhagavatam with contemporary presentation and delivery, as well as being a book for the introspective and thoughtful reader, make this a most wonderful offering at the feet of Srila Prabhupada, in whose footsteps we all pray to follow in.

I highly recommend curious and interested readers to absorb the contents of these pages, and share them with those who have great meaning in your life [so] the benefit multiplies!

I would like to wish a warm thank you to Gauranga Darshan Das, and the editorial and publishing teams involved in the production of this book. I wish you all success and look forward to reading more books like this'—Alfred Brush Ford, great-grandson of Henry Ford and chairman, Temple of the Vedic Planetarium

'*Dhruva* is an engaging journey of enlightenment. Prepare to be captivated as Gauranga Darshan Das unveils the transformative power of "philosophical counselling" in this awe-inspiring narrative. Brace yourself for a thought-provoking exploration, as the author's brilliance shines through every page, with his profound insights on relationships and success. This enthralling adventure will illuminate your perspectives and resonate deeply within your soul'—Gauranga Das, director of Govardhan Ecovillage, ISKCON GBC, author and speaker

'I believe that learning lessons from our ancient texts, such as the Srimad Bhagavatam, is essential for the younger generation. Dhruva is one of the most revered and beloved characters from the ancient texts. Many people hold him in high esteem, considering him a role model and a tremendous source of inspiration when it comes to demonstrating unwavering determination.

I am very impressed by the way author Gauranga Darshan Das masterfully highlighted several effective tools for enlivening relationships and achieving enduring success in his book, *Dhruva*, through captivating narrative, leaving a lasting impact on the readers'—Vijay Bhatkar, Padma Bhushan awardee and founder, chancellor and chief mentor, Multiversity

'Gauranga Darshan Das's engaging narration of Dhruva's inspiring journey towards real success is sure to inspire you in yours'—Jay Shetty, #1 *New York Times* bestselling author, podcast host and purpose coach

'Intense drama, practical wisdom, gripping narration and scriptural authenticity come together in Gauranga Darshan's *Dhruva*'—Vivek Bindra, CEO and founder, Bada Business Pvt. Ltd

'Dhruva is said to be at the very centre of the galaxy. By reflecting deeply on his fascinating story, Gauranga Darshan Das offers readers a profound and inspirational philosophy for life as well as practical ways of nourishing successful relationships'—David Haberman, professor of religious studies at Indiana University

'The mighty emotions of young prince Dhruva and his journey to success presented by Gauranga Darshan Das are sure to stay with the reader forever'—Ashishkumar Chauhan, managing director and CEO, National Stock Exchange of India

'*Dhruva* is an amalgamation of drama, happiness, realization, understanding, victory through actions and attitudes as Gauranga Darshan Das takes us through an enchanting narration of Dhruva's odyssey to success despite challenges in relationship. A must-read success and relationship playbook'—Karthik Ramesh, chief growth officer, TaskBench

'Dhruva is an adored character and a role model for success for many in this world. Gauranga Darshan Das's engaging narration of Dhruva's journey to success, intertwined with profound insights into relationships, is sure to captivate and enchant your heart'—Hrishikesh Mafatlal, chairman and chief executive of the Arvind Mafatlal Group of Companies

'In a world full of complexities, author Gauranga Darshan Das has made an extraordinary effort to enlighten readers with simple and easily applicable lessons for a successful and fulfilling life, while embarking on a journey towards spirituality'—Neeraj Choksi, founder, NJ Group

'As an entrepreneur, my journey of sustaining meaningful and productive relationships and discovering different definitions of success has led me to seek inspiration from Gauranga Darshan Das, a sage monk and an exceptional spiritual teacher. His book *Dhruva* will captivate you with profound insights and practical wisdom on achieving success and fostering meaningful relationships. Weaved into the incredible tales of Prince Dhruva, there are life lessons that can give us a new perspective on responsibility, happiness, determination, leadership and most importantly, acceptance of success and failure. May this book ignite our purpose and guide us towards completeness'—Jignesh Desai, co-founder, NJ Group

'*Dhruva* is yet another marvel where Gauranga Darshan Das explores the intricacies of relationships and success while sharing with the reader "pearls of wisdom" that actually work in practical life'—Shubha Vilas, author, educationalist, life coach and storyteller

ALSO BY THE SAME AUTHOR

Study Guides

Gītā Subodhinī
Īśopanishad Subodhinī
Upadeśāmrta Subodhinī
Bhakti Rasāmṛta Subodhinī
Caitanya Subodhinī (4 Volumes)
Bhāgavata Subodhinī (10 volumes)
The Art of Studying & Teaching Scriptures

Self-enrichment Books

Bhāgavata Pravāha
Caitanya Pravāha
Gita, The Jewel Box
Answers to Life's Questions
Disapproved But Not Disowned

Illustrated Children Books

Gita Wisdom Tales (5 volumes)
Bhagavatam Tales (5 volumes)
Ramayana to Inspire Young Minds

Shloka Books

Gītā Ratnamālā
Caitanya Ratnamālā
Bhāgavata Tattvamālā
Bhāgavata Ratnamālā (2 volumes)

DHRUVA

RELATIONSHIP *and* SUCCESS SUTRAS *from the* STORY *of a* CELEBRATED PRINCE

GAURANGA DARSHAN DAS

PENGUIN
ANANDA
An imprint of Penguin Random House

PENGUIN ANANDA

USA | Canada | UK | Ireland | Australia
New Zealand | India | South Africa | China | Singapore

Penguin Ananda is part of the Penguin Random House group of companies whose addresses can be found at global.penguinrandomhouse.com

Published by Penguin Random House India Pvt. Ltd
4th Floor, Capital Tower 1, MG Road,
Gurugram 122 002, Haryana, India

First published in Penguin Ananda by Penguin Random House India 2023

10 9 8 7 6 5 4 3 2 1

ISBN 9780143463597

Typeset in Sabon by Manipal Technologies Limited, Manipal

www.penguin.co.in

To my dear parents, by whose culture
I became inclined to spirituality

To my beloved guru, by whose blessings
I am what I am today in my spiritual life

To Srila Prabhupada, by whose books
I am nourished with spiritual wisdom

To all the readers and seekers who aspire
to enliven their lives with timeless wisdom

Contents

SECTION II
AN EFFICIENT EMPEROR

Introduction

Generally, readers skip a book's introduction and preface—I have done that several times myself as a reader. But it was only when I started writing that I realized how vital a part they are of a book. In truth, it takes more time and effort to write an introduction to a book than a chapter. This is because the former addresses the following questions:

What was the need to write the book? What exactly is the essential message of the treatise? Allow me to walk you through the answers to these questions.

From the frigid ice caps of the Antarctic to the rugged deserts of the Middle East, meeting someone who doesn't hanker for 'organic relationships' and 'enduring success' is more than simply a challenge. Each of us desire nourishing relationships, but how easy are they to establish? Countless people strive for success in life, but how many identify what true success is and how it can be attained?

Browsing through some tips on success and relationships may be of much help, but what if you had the chance to learn them from the life of a leader? Wouldn't that be most insightful and practical? Analysing the subtle aspects of familial and friendly relationships can also reveal lessons that live on in our hearts for the future. Though this treatise, I humbly attempt to do the same.

But who is Dhruva and why delve deeper into his life? The wonderful story of our hero Dhruva appears in the magnum opus Srimad Bhagavatam written by sage Vyasa. This book is a detailed narration of Prince Dhruva's life right from his childhood until he is flown to Dhruvaloka, the Pole Star. In this enthralling journey, you will surely find jewel-like sutras for success and relationships. With the flip of each page, you will decode those encrypted sutras, which when applied, will open the doors to true success and meaningful relationships. The activities and attitudes of the various personalities in this story uncover amazing insights on wholesome relations and the keys for success that can be applied.

How is a discussion on relationships relevant and important? An earthen pot, once broken, is not reusable. Even if one manages to put the broken pieces of the pot together and make it usable again, one has to be extremely careful while handling the pot. It has to be cared for more than a pot that has been freshly made. The slightest mishandling of such a repaired pot breaks it and makes it permanently irreparable. Relationships also resemble such a pot. If one is insensitive in terms of one's speech and dealings, it could lead to the breaking of someone's heart forever and beyond repair. Learning from Dhruva's story, the dynamics of relationships and the nature of speech that makes them or breaks them is exciting.

What about success? A student who obtains marvellous grades in his examinations by cheating may seem successful, but his real understanding of the subject is exposed with time. On the other hand, an honest and hard-working student might get average grades, but his genuine understanding of the subject is sure to help him in the future. Success attained through duplicity and unfair means may artificially boost one's ego, but success achieved by honesty and integrity satisfies the heart everlastingly. It's the inner values of a person that make success satisfactory and sustainable, not its showy appearance and fame.

Apart from this, some people attribute success to one's destiny or fate, popularly known as the law of karma, while some say that it's a product of one's sincere efforts. How much is one's success or failure dependent on karma? Can destiny be changed? What's the role of spirituality in this? My purpose is to address these questions through this book. I also wish to bring to the reader's notice that apart from learning how to attain success, we also need to learn how to deal with failure—after all, life offers both, and we need to be realistic and not idealistic.

In this book, I attempt to analyse the essential rubric of relationships, provide guidance on how to achieve enduring success and highlight ways of dealing with setbacks and emotional outbursts, through an engaging narration that meanders through the life of Dhruva and has been split into two sections.

Section I: Dhruva was the son of a virtuous mother, Suniti, who happened to be a neglected queen of King Uttanapada. Proud Suruchi, the second wife of the king, was his favourite. Once, Suruchi's harsh speech and Uttanapada's neglect wounded the tender heart of the five-year-old Dhruva, who left home and entered the forest to fulfil his ambition. What was his ambition and how he did he succeed in fulfilling it? What providential support did he receive? What were his feelings after having attained his goal? The answers to these questions form the first section of this book. The main characters in this success story of young Dhruva, namely Suniti, Suruchi, Uttanapada, Narada Muni and, of course, Lord Vishnu himself, reveal several sutras for good relationships, including an analysis of common human emotions and emotional outbursts. The determined endeavours of Dhruva elucidate several sutras for success. This part also presents the transformative stories of Uttanapada and Suruchi and how a family built on strained relationships was strung together in a loving bond.

Section II: This part describes Dhruva's activities as an emperor and specifically his emotional outburst when his brother was killed by a Yaksha. While he was initially successful in defeating the Yakshas in a fierce battle, he found himself dumbstruck when they overpowered him with their illusions. How did he overcome them? Did someone help him during that hour of crisis? After overcoming his opponent, his rage somehow got out of control. Was there someone who could calm him down? And in the end, how efficiently did he rule his empire and eventually attain Dhruvaloka? I invite you to fish out the answers to these questions from the book's second part. The chief characters of this part, namely the sages Svayambhuva Manu and Kuvera and their dealings with Dhruva, reveal another set of wonderful relationship and success sutras. Dhruva's exemplary rule and retirement are rich with lessons on leadership, responsibility and detachment.

Of all the wonderful stories in Srimad Bhagavatam, I have chosen the story of Dhruva to narrate, because its multiple characters and their personality traits reveal great life lessons on several universally relevant subjects. A careful analysis of this ancient story reveals brilliant insights into enlivening emotions and relationships between wife and husband; general dealings with younger ones, elders and colleagues; positivity; unburying the qualities of sensitivity, empathy, love and honest repentance, and especially a mother's love and child's gratitude.

I bring to you through this text the methods of 'philosophical counselling' amidst the confusions that everyone faces in life. It was our hero Dhruva who was exposed to the philosophical counselling of his mother Suniti, his guru Narada Muni and his grandfather Svayambhuva Manu. His different responses to the counsels given by these three well-wishing elders leave us with heart-warming lessons on honesty and flexibility.

At the end of each chapter is a set of quick but practical sutras for success and enlivening friendships—

the 'pearls of wisdom'—that you will be able to apply in life's ever-changing situations. Thus, I pray that you travel through the pages of this work and find organic relationships and perennial success as they await your arrival at the last leaf.

Gauranga Darshan Das
Govardhan Ecovillage
4 May 2023

SECTION I

A DETERMINED PRINCE

1

A Sliced-Up Heart

Building cordial relationships requires speech that is pleasant to the ears and the heart. Speak sweet, and we'll delight the hearts of those we meet.

'You have no right to sit on your father's lap,' thundered Suruchi. Piercing through the eardrums of a five-year-old Dhruva, this statement, like a razor-edged cleaver, sliced up his tender heart. These words were indeed queen Suruchi's envy, disguised in her speech.

'Why am I being forbidden from sitting on my father's lap while my brother Uttama merrily enjoys there? What is my mistake?' These thoughts dampened prince Dhruva's spirits and left him confused. Although nervous, he tried to make sense of the whole situation.

But Suruchi wanted to hit out at Dhruva, so she continued. 'Although you are also the king's son, you cannot sit on his lap or throne, because you are not born of me. You have taken birth from another woman's womb. Being a mere child, you do not understand the difference between me and your mother, Suniti. But you better get this right. It is me who your father is fond of, not your mother.' Using her words indiscriminately, Suruchi bruised the tender heart of the little prince, Dhruva.

Words can make relationships and break them too. Insensitive speech adds the letter 's' to 'words' making them 'swords'. Carefully tasting the bitter words we use would prevent any need to eat them later.

If cordial relationships are one's priority, then curtailing the urge to speak harshly is compulsory.

Two Contrasting Characters under the Same Roof

The childhood innocence of Dhruva couldn't identify the difference between his mother, Suniti and his stepmother, Suruchi. But the envy with which Suruchi lashed out at Dhruva proclaimed volumes of distinction.

Although both Suniti and Suruchi were the queens of King Uttanapada, the treatment they received was visibly different. While Uttanapada showered his affection on his younger wife, Suruchi, he forsook his elder queen Suniti and her son Dhruva.

Suniti bore a virtuous character but was still deprived of her husband's warmth. Yet, tolerance, soft-heartedness, empathy, sympathy and many such qualities had found their abode in her. Above all, she was a great devotee of Lord Vishnu.

In stark contrast, Suruchi was proud, haughty and oppressive. Binding Uttanapada with her femininity and possessiveness, she reduced him to a henpecked husband. She wanted all the love of Uttanapada only for her son, Uttama.

Suruchi knew that the throne would pass down to Dhruva as a part of his inheritance since he was older than Suruchi's child, Uttama, the only other son of the king. However, Suruchi desired to reserve the throne for Uttama. To do so, she would have to distance Dhruva from the love and care of King Uttanapada right from his boyhood. Thus, being tightly gripped by selfishness and envy, Suruchi unhesitatingly chastised young Dhruva.

Envy is the most undesirable quality that disrupts relationships to the core. An envious person cannot tolerate others' superiority over oneself and always tries to pull others down.

The Henpecked Husband of a Haughty Queen

King Uttanapada was not an ordinary person. He was the great-grandson of Lord Brahma himself. Despite coming from such a great lineage, Uttanapada's family wasn't happy. In fact, several tensions were brewing within the royal palace.

To put it in terms of cricket, what happens if an umpire sides with the team he prefers and thereby gives partial decisions? Well, the wronged would surely start fuming, wouldn't they?

King Uttanapada somehow missed out on this important principle that we find even in modern-day sports. A king is supposed to treat all his citizens equally and a father is supposed to treat all his children equally. Isn't he? Uttanapada was both a king, a father and a husband, but he terribly failed at fulfilling his responsibilities. He was overly attached to Suruchi, his younger wife while he neglected his first wife, Suniti. To top that, he drenched Uttama with his love while he hesitated to put Dhruva on his lap.

In truth, he did love both of his sons, but his inclination towards Suruchi overrode his fatherly feelings for Dhruva. Uttanapada wasn't ignorant of what treatment one must give to one's children or wives. He consciously neglected Suniti and her son, for he was victimized by his own undue attachment—a folly that would immerse him in an ocean of remorsefulness in the time to come.

We become weaker than ourselves when we succumb to undue attachments and unfair obligations.

A person with a weak heart loses all discrimination and gives in to temptations. Temptations give immediate pleasure but they result in long-term plight.

Dealing with Younger Ones

That day, while being seated on the royal throne, Uttanapada lovingly hosted Uttama on his lap. With great love, he caressed the young lad when Dhruva, his elder son, happened to pass by. Seeing his father affectionately pat his stepbrother, Dhruva too desired to relish loving exchanges with his father. So, he entered the royal hall with great anticipation. Running towards his father, he expected an affectionate embrace. But soon, his excitement fizzled out, for all he got was a cold reception from his father. Moreover, his stepmother also showered upon him the choicest of rude remarks.

> *Our dealings with young ones shape their mindset. A love-laden heart coupled with sensitive speech will enable us to bring out the best in them.*

Harsh and insensitive behaviours of elders could form deep negative impressions on children. Therefore, elders need to be responsible for the children's healthy emotional growth, especially during their formative years.

Every child is rightfully entitled to the love of his or her father—it takes no rulebook to understand this. But unfortunately, selfishness had blinded Suruchi to the innocent emotions of little Dhruva. With Suruchi's greed and possessiveness in play, Dhruva was openly denied his father's love, and of course, the throne to which he was a rightful heir. Things would've been different for Dhruva had Suruchi been more empathetic.

When Pride and Envy Overpower

While Uttanapada mutely listened, jealous Suruchi barged out at the prince, 'Dhruva, your desire to sit on your father's lap will not be fulfilled. But if you still wish so, then you better worship Lord Vishnu, and by His boon, be born as my son in your next life. Only then would you get the privilege of sitting on the king's lap.'

Pride and envy had arrested Suruchi. She considered herself superior to her co-wife and the authorizer of her husband's love. She considered taking birth from her womb to be a great privilege to the extent that it would require a boon from Lord Vishnu! The ancient wisdom texts teach us that by worshipping the Lord, one would be free from the repeated cycle of birth and death in this world and reach the Lord's eternal abode where birth, disease, old age and death are absent. So, why would any sincere worshipper of Lord Vishnu take birth from the womb of an arrogant woman like Suruchi?

Attributing too much of self-importance and being too self-righteous makes one oblivious to the obvious and oppressive towards the innocent.

Did you observe another interesting aspect of Suruchi's harsh speech? Despite her swelling with pride and arrogance, she recommended that Dhruva worship Lord Vishnu. So, does that mean she was a great devotee of Lord Vishnu and had great faith in Him?

Unfortunately not! She made such statements only to impress Uttanapada with her pretentious devotion (*bhakti*) so as to increase Uttanapada's attachment to her. She desired her husband to think in this way: 'My younger queen is not only beautiful but is also spiritually elevated! I am so fortunate to have such a wife.'

> *Those brimming with hypocrisy spend most of their time finding others' faults and flaunting their flawlessness.*

Suruchi was envious of Suniti. And now that envy was also being directed to Dhruva. Her misbehaviour towards Dhruva would surely pain Suniti and offer some egoistic pleasure to Suruchi's heart. This is another downside of envy.

> *Envy is contagious. The long arms of envy eventually trap others in the same net as the object of envy.*

Uncontrolled envious 'thoughts' eventually take form as sharp 'words' and mature as destructive 'actions'. When undetected, envy spreads like wildfire and turns relationships into nightmares.

When a Leader Is Silent about Injustice

All this time, Suruchi had been verbalizing her poisonous mentality and unreasonably admonishing Dhruva, while Uttanapada preferred to be silent. How could a father tolerate someone misbehaving with his son? Also, how could a king silently ignore injustice taking place right before him? Well, King Uttanapada really lowered the bar. He didn't say or do anything to stop Suruchi.

On the contrary, his muteness supported and implicitly approved Suruchi's misbehaviour. He neither welcomed Dhruva nor intercepted Suruchi. As a father, he didn't even try consoling Dhruva.

> *Observing irresponsible behaviour and overlooking it, despite having the ability to decimate it, is sheer irresponsibility.*

Suruchi felt confident in speaking harshly because she knew Uttanapada favoured her. The undue lenience Uttanapada gave her made her impudent and gave her the confidence to speak and act according to her whims. Being dear to a great person may invoke pride in the heart of the endeared. As a result, they may look down upon those who do not have such a privilege and that's what Suruchi was doing now. As the father of Dhruva, timely intervention from Uttanapada could have prevented the situation from worsening but his vow of silence only added fuel to the fire.

> *Our timely intervention in the lives of the young ones would set things straight in their lives and ours too.*

Loneliness amidst Crowd

While Suruchi's harsh words minced Dhruva's delicate heart, Uttanapada's silence added insult to injury. Seeing how the king and the queen treated the boy, the palace residents kept silent. How could they confront the king or the queen? After all, they were their subordinates. Thus, although Dhruva was clearly being mistreated, no one dared to pacify him.

> *Some of the greatest painful moments in life are those when we have no one to console us in a distressful situation.*

Where would a disheartened Dhruva take refuge? Dhruva's tender heart had already been inflicted with the blows of insensitive behaviour. Battling with the struggles of life single-handedly requires great wisdom and maturity. Even experienced people fail to reconcile a bewildering situation, what to expect of an inexperienced child? Dhruva experienced a sense of 'loneliness' while situated in the magnificent royal palace amidst several facilities, servants, soldiers and even the king and the queen! He didn't know how to respond.

Dhruva's fragile heart had been axed and his desire had been thwarted. Shattered by the force of his stepmother's harsh words and disappointed by his father's silence, he breathed heavily in anger, just like a snake that has been struck with a stick. As a young courageous *kshatriya*, with royal blood flowing in his veins, tolerating such an insult was impossible for him.

Weeping in depression, Dhruva ran to his mother, Suniti. How do you think Suniti would respond to this situation? Until then, she had been personally experiencing neglect by her husband. She had tolerated the pride and envy of her co-wife. But now her little son, the object of her love, had also been wronged by them. What would she do now? Would she confront Suruchi or Uttanapada and fight for justice? Or would she just tolerate it silently? How would her response impact Dhruva? Flip the page to find out.

* * *

Pearls of Wisdom

Relationship Sutras

1. Restrict the urge to speak stiffly and raise the intensity to speak sweetly.
2. Using pleasing words can make a wonderful world within you. Why not be happy free of cost?
3. When you envy others for what they have, you forget what you have. So, beware of envy.
4. Replacing superiority complex with sensitivity and envy with appreciation wins us more friends.
5. Get rid of pride by recognizing how blessed others are. Dismiss envy by seeing how blessed you are.
6. Cut the invisible ropes of undue attachments with the axe of impartiality.
7. Injustice is easy to serve but hard to digest.
8. Loneliness reminds us of the company we had and that which we need.
9. Let's allow others to thrive instead of being oppressive.
10. Try to see good in others instead of holding onto self-righteousness.
11. Don't look down upon those who do not have the privileges you have.
12. Replace bias and partiality with grace and responsibility.
13. Don't ignore your responsibility to protect your dependants, at least when you can.

2

Three Golden Pieces of Advice from a Glorious Mother

Duly acknowledging and empathizing with the feelings of those in pain, instead of dismissing them, makes our hearts grow bigger and their hearts brighter.

Dhruva's emotions were soaring; being a five-year-old child, they burst forth. With his maturity still ripening, coming to terms with the situation at hand was too difficult for him. To Dhruva, this wasn't simply some embarrassment but much more than that. His blood boiled in a fire of rage. He wanted to avenge Suruchi's insult and was determined to teach her a good lesson.

Bitter feelings towards Uttama, his stepbrother, had begun to emerge in Dhruva's heart. Although Uttama was simply sitting on his father's lap without hurting Dhruva, he still became an object of Dhruva's envy. After all, he was sitting in a position that Dhruva desired.

Wailing in pain, smouldering in anger and hissing like a serpent, Dhruva proceeded to his mother, Suniti, as she sombrely awaited his arrival whilst being seated in her palace amidst several servants. Of what use are an opulent palace, lavish facilities and numerous servants when the people we love are indifferent to us?

The news of the incident had already reached Suniti before Dhruva's arrival. The neglectful behaviour of Uttanapada was already something Suniti was dealing with. Now, seeing her son experience the same pain, her grief surpassed all boundaries.

Eventually, when Dhruva reached out to his mother for solace and shelter, Suniti lifted and placed him on her lap as tears kept rolling down his cheeks. Losing her patience, she began lamenting and thinking harsh words for her co-wife. She was consumed by grief, just like a forest creeper that is eaten up by a wildfire. Tears cascaded down her lotus-like eyes. How can a mother tolerate the pain of her beloved child?

Suniti began breathing heavily. A remedy for the painful situation was beyond the reach of her thoughts. She was not a person who was interested in confrontation and complaints. However, being a glorious lady and a great devotee of Lord Vishnu, she was equipped with the maturity to handle the situation. She detected great disappointment in Dhruva—the reason he developed revengeful thoughts towards Suruchi and Uttama. She could sympathize and empathize with his emotions.

Appropriate emotional support given at the right time facilitates deep, long-lasting relationships.

Although it wasn't difficult for Suniti to understand her son's feelings, she prioritized the elimination of the overwhelming negativity in his impressionable heart. She considered subduing the revengeful thoughts in Dhruva's mind to be her primary responsibility. Thus, she spoke some wise words to pacify her son.

Empathizing with others' problems is important in relationships but, instead of just stopping there, one should also attempt to bring them towards a solution.

Negativity, when dwelled upon, only increases; Trying to divert the mind toward something positive makes the situation less painful and more hopeful.

First Piece of Gold

Suniti told Dhruva, 'My dear son, please don't wish ill fortune for others, even though they have caused you pain.'

What did Suniti mean by this?—Should Dhruva not desire any harm for impolite Suruchi, the one who insulted him causelessly? The one who deprived Dhruva of his natural right to sit on his father's lap?—Yes, that's exactly what Suniti said.

Tolerating the trivial inconveniences others cause can make us tranquil, transform them in time, and leave a trail for others to tread.

This was the point Suniti was making. But to Dhruva who was fuming with a kshatriya spirit, this did not make much sense—he thought it was reasonable to maintain anger and revengeful thoughts against someone like Suruchi.

Second Piece of Gold

Suniti's second statement was: 'Dear child, please understand that anyone who inflicts pain upon others suffers oneself from that pain.'

Did this indicate that Suruchi's wreaking of pain upon Dhruva and Suniti meant that Suruchi would suffer too, in the future? Even without Dhruva having to desire or act to harm her?—No. The essence of what Suniti spoke was simply this: 'We must have inflicted pain upon someone in the past and that pain is coming back to us through Suruchi.'

Suniti's words reflected the reactionary chain of karma. Her spontaneous statements have profound meanings that can be soaked into our lives practically. We often blame, criticize and accuse others who have caused us pain through their words or actions. Of course, sometimes it is necessary to do so but there's something more significant that we need to understand from the situation.

For instance, a thief needs to be pointed out and be duly punished for his theft. The punishment given to a thief is a reaction to his thievery and is meant to prevent him from stealing in the future. But does the punishment given to the thief fully compensate for the pain of the one duped? Although the victim may be pacified when they get their money back, the delay in retrieving the money would have left them worried and stressed. Isn't it?

Now, let's try peeling the skin of the scenario and get to its core.

Why, in the first place, did the thief steal only from this person out of millions of other prospective victims?—One answer is karma—the reaction to one's past deeds, often called destiny or fate. Every action in this world results in a positive or negative reaction, depending on its nature. We reap the results of our actions through different agents—this is karma. Thus, the thief could be considered an instrument of the victim's karma. This understanding, however, in no way minimizes the need to catch and punish the thief. A wrongdoer must be punished according to the severity of the misdeeds committed.

What the thief did was undoubtedly criminal, and the reaction to what he did would certainly embrace him when dispensed by authorized agents. But Suniti's second statement highlighted the victim's balance of pain due to past misdeeds. This balance was settled via the medium of the thief.

The laws of nature and the expert administration of Almighty God ensure that every wrongdoer experiences the reaction to their wrongdoings through various persons or situations. These may occur immediately or much later, perhaps even in another lifetime.*

---

*This discussion doesn't end here, although we table it for now in order to maintain contextual relevance. Someone may naturally

> *Externally addressing the situations in life as far as humanly possible while internally reconciling them philosophically brings a harmonious balance to life.*

The extent to which one must address a situation depends on the extent to which one has been wronged, and one's ability and preference to deal with it. While some people wish to aggressively fight for justice, others may effortlessly forgive and tolerate it.

In this case, the mother and son had different ways of responding to the situation. Suniti chose to forgive and tolerate the pain caused by Suruchi and taught Dhruva to do the same. But Suruchi's insulting remarks only spawned the seeds of revenge in Dhruva's heart.

> *Life's situations are often not within our control but our response is.*

Thus, the first two pieces of advice Suniti gave Dhruva didn't appeal to his heart, which was throbbing with pain. Fuelled by passion, he was determined to prove his superiority to Suruchi.

Others may trouble us but sometimes the trouble may simply be the fruit cultivated by our past karma. Such fruits may be offered to us by others or those we've offended—above all, they're simply the Lord's

---

question, 'If everything is *predestined*, where is my *independence* and *freewill*? Can I change my destiny?—essentially, 'Yes but conditions apply!' Please turn to Chapter 9 for a further analysis of this subject.

arrangement. So, refusing them is impossible. Therefore, we must not hate their giver.

The Third Piece of Gold

Suniti then provided a third piece of advice to Dhruva. She said, 'My dear boy, whatever your stepmother said is a fact. Your father does not consider me to be his wife or even his maidservant. He feels ashamed to accept me. You are born of an unfortunate woman and have been bred by her milk. Although Suruchi's words were harsh to hear, she did say something worthwhile. She told you to worship Lord Vishnu to fulfil your desire of sitting on your father's lap or throne, just like your stepbrother. My dear son Dhruva, you better follow this advice. Whatever desire you may have, you should worship Lord Vishnu and give up your envious attitude. Only He can fulfil all your wishes.'

Thus, instead of accusing Suruchi or Uttanapada, Suniti maturely directed Dhruva toward the shelter of Lord Vishnu. When others hurt us, it is difficult to identify any good in their words or actions. But Suniti told Dhruva that Suruchi's statement about the Lord's worship was true. She valued this statement over the other offensive statements Suruchi made. She bore no hatred against Suruchi, who hated her so bitterly.

It's liberating to be an essence-seeker rather than a nonsense-hater.

Recommending devotion (bhakti) unto Lord Vishnu, Suniti further instructed, 'Dear Dhruva, your father was the son of Svayambhuva Manu, who was the son of Lord Brahma, who was born from Lord Vishnu at the beginning of the creation. Only by worshipping Lord Vishnu could your great-grandfather Brahma create the universe and your grandfather Manu achieve happiness and liberation so efficiently. Thus, it is only by worshipping Lord Vishnu that your desires will be fulfilled too. So, please take His shelter. He is very kind to His devotees. So, keep Him in your heart and perform bhakti without deviation.'

The inappropriate behaviour of others can induce negative feelings in us but, in truth, we would be the first victims of such negativity if we don't consciously nudge ourselves toward positivity. When someone comes to us with an agitated mind, we shouldn't speak in such a way that aggravates their negativity. Rather, we should try bringing them towards positivity.

Expressing her deep devotion to Lord Vishnu, the glorious mother Suniti concluded, 'Dear Dhruva, I can only give you the affection of one mother, but the love the Lord bathes His devotees with, is more than the affection of millions of mothers put together. No one else can extinguish your distress except the lotus-eyed Lord Vishnu. Even goddess Lakshmi, eagerly worshipped by several *devatas* for their good fortune, keenly serves Him alone.' Suniti being a great devotee, thus handled the situation with great maturity. Wise people can deal with life's testing situations maturely and transfer this maturity to others, thus elevating their consciousness.

> *Maturity is the ability to convert a negative situation into a positive opportunity to grow in life and thus inch forward to God.*

Hope in Hopeless Situations

Mistreating others or being mishandled by others is common in life. This may take form in one's words or behaviour, intentionally or even unintentionally. Blaming, arguing and lamenting are natural reactions in a calamitous situation but one should outgrow that stage and maturely consider the best course of action. There is one thing that is unthinkably the most prudent thing to do—take the Lord's shelter along with doing whatever is humanly possible.

> *One will find hope in the most hopeless situation simply by taking shelter of God.*

Our good consciousness can be positively impactful while our poor attitude can negatively influence others. This was indeed how Suniti and Suruchi were different.

While Suruchi's pride and Uttanapada's irresponsibility pained Dhruva's heart, virtuous Suniti's good counsel gave him hope and inspiration. Although Suruchi hated Suniti and insulted her son, Suniti never grudged or envied Suruchi or her son Uttama. On the contrary, being a pure-hearted lady, she tried to calm Dhruva down with some advice of peace.

Although Suniti advised Dhruva not to be envious of Suruchi, Dhruva still harboured anger and the desire to avenge Suruchi's misbehaviour—this could be attributed to his innate nature as a kshatriya prince. Therefore, Dhruva couldn't digest his mother's first two pieces of advice. But did he agree with her third advice on worshipping Lord Vishnu to fulfil his wishes? What exactly was his wish at this moment? Turn the page to know the answers.

* * *

Pearls of Wisdom

Relationship Sutras

1. We derive emotional satisfaction by giving emotional support to others when they need it the most.
2. Empathizing with others' problems is good but attempting to find solutions is great.
3. Be an essence-seeker, not a nonsense-hater.
4. Strike conversations that create hope and positivity while keeping negativity outside the gate.
5. Negativity is like seeing dark clouds. Positivity is like embracing the rain. Make your choice.
6. Let's be wise to seek opportunities to grow amidst reversals and inspire others to do so.
7. Finding hope in hopeless situations is indeed a herculean task. Why not seek help from the One who arranged it all?
8. Let other's misbehaviour not stimulate our ill-behaviour.
9. When you see good in others, you replicate the way God sees you.
10. Try to tolerate the trivial inconveniences others cause instead of over-reacting.
11. Don't overly blame the instrument of your karma.

3

Determination Tested

One who is fixed up in one's resolve despite all tests and temptations is the candidate eligible for success.

Although Suniti's first two pieces of advice didn't appeal much to Dhruva, he took the third one seriously. He liked the idea of worshipping Lord Vishnu to fulfil his heart's desire. But what was his desire now? The denial he received regarding sitting on his father's lap had spurred within his heart the desire to acquire a much greater position.

Tormented by Suruchi's wounding words, Dhruva's ambition to prove his greatness steadily escalated. He thought, 'I must attain a position superior to even my great grandfather Brahma's.' After deliberate consideration, Dhruva equipped himself with riveted determination and headed to the forest, leaving the palace's comforts behind. He wanted to please Lord Vishnu, who would grant his wish.

Mere lamentation upon facing a reversal is not beneficial and one must find a means to mitigate such lamentation.

Dhruva desired to worship and meditate on Lord Vishnu without much understanding of the Lord's glory. However, his indomitable determination to avenge his stepmother's behaviour outweighed his bhakti to the Lord.

Lord Vishnu, who dwells in the hearts of all living beings as the Supersoul or *Parmatma*, naturally understands everyone's intentions. Despite knowing the motives of Dhruva in approaching Him, the all-merciful Father of all beings Vishnu, only thought of the boy's benefit.

An Unexpected Meeting

As prince Dhruva entered deeper into the forest, before him appeared the great sage Narada Muni with a veena in his hands. Narada Muni was a great devotee of Lord Vishnu and a wise sage who could look through the three phases of time—past, present and future. Moreover, he had the special ability to read the minds of the people that he met.

Was that simply a coincidence? Well, it surely appeared to be. However, there was a perfect arrangement behind the visible scenes. Lord Vishnu knew the reason behind the little prince's departure from the palace and his arrival in the forest. To guide the inexperienced boy in his worship and meditation, the Lord inspired one of His dear devotees Narada Muni to meet and mentor him.

The Lord is boundlessly compassionate, for He personally arranges all the support and guidance required by the one who sincerely seeks Him.

Sage Narada understood how Dhruva had been humiliated in the palace and could envision his intentions of attaining a position superior to Brahma. Narada marvelled at Dhruva's determination and thought, 'How wonderful is the nature of the kshatriyas! They cannot tolerate even the slightest infringement of their prestige. This boy is just five years old, yet he left his father's palace, being so affected by the harsh words of his stepmother!'

An Unsolicited Counsel

Thinking thus, Narada Muni approached Dhruva. He touched the boy's head with his all-virtuous hand and spoke thus. 'My dear child, why did you come to the forest alone? This place is filled with ferocious animals. Are you not fearful?'

Little Dhruva's demeanour didn't reveal the slightest fear; instead, it proclaimed his unshakeable determination. Narada continued, 'Why did you take your stepmother's rude words so seriously? You are only a little boy and should just be absorbed in playing. What difference can a child understand between honour and insult?'

But Dhruva's juggernaut of determination was irrepressible. Involving himself in childish play would not dilute the effect of the insult he had been subjected to. The insult had been engraved on his tender heart and only avenging it would give him some relief.

Understanding his mind, Narada said, 'My dear Dhruva, if you are mature enough to understand the difference between honour and insult, then please understand this: Everyone in this world faces the results of one's previous actions and thus encounters enjoyment or suffering, honour or dishonour. This is the arrangement of the Supreme Lord. A wise person faces all these experiences without getting overly effected.'

> *A sober person is not unduly affected by the inevitable dualities of this world.*

Narada Muni's words were similar to Suniti's. Formerly, she had explained to Dhruva how one experiences happiness or distress according to one's own deeds through others and that is why one shouldn't hate the instrument of one's own karma. But these words spoken by his beloved mother and later repeated by the great sage didn't appeal to Dhruva, for he was overcome with ambition and a revengeful attitude.

A Test for Determination

To test Dhruva's determination in fulfilling his ambition, Narada Muni said, 'Dear child, now you have decided to worship Lord Vishnu in the forest and meditate on him, as advised by your mother. But I think it would be difficult for you to perform austerities to please Vishnu. Satisfying Him is a daunting task. Even great sages performed thousands of years of meditation and some even for many lifetimes, only desiring to get a glimpse of Him, but they didn't succeed. How can a mere child like you possibly please Him and fulfil your wish? Therefore, my dear boy, you should not endeavour for this—you will not be successful. Better go home. When you grow up, you may try to worship the Lord in the forest.'

> *One's resolve may be tested at any moment by anyone. The one who passes such tests by being fully fixed up on one's goals without deviation is sure to attain success.*

Imbuing his conversation with philosophy, Narada further counselled Dhruva, 'One should try to keep oneself satisfied in any condition of life—whether happiness or distress—whatever one encounters by the arrangement of God. One who endures the dualities of this world is ultimately eligible for liberation.' Despite hearing this, Dhruva's determination remained immovable. Returning home was not even in his frame of thought. He would please Lord Vishnu no matter what obstacles the fierce forest would pose.

Three Keys to Healthy Relationships

To educate the child in the art of dealing with people in this world, Narada Muni said, 'Dear boy, we meet three kinds of people in life—those who are more qualified than us, those who are equally qualified and those who are less qualified than us. In other words, they are our seniors, equals and juniors in some way. By learning the fine art of approaching and interacting with them, we can avoid facing unpleasant circumstances. Therefore, to remain unaffected in your dealings with these three categories of people, follow these three golden principles.'

1. 'When you meet someone more qualified than you, be happy instead of being envious.'
2. 'When you meet someone less qualified than yourself, be kind instead of being oppressive.'
3. 'And when you meet someone equal to you, befriend them, instead of competing with them.'

Narada Muni's profound words give us three great keys to healthy relationships. This is the smart art of dealing with the three kinds of people we meet. Whoever we meet in this world surely belongs to one of these three categories. If everyone deals with others in line with these three keys, conflicts could be easily kept at bay and cordial relationships would be established, which in turn would nourish our hearts. But how did Dhruva receive them?

Narada Muni's teachings on karma, the will of God and the art of dealing with people—none of them appealed to the mind of ambitious Dhruva. Overwhelmed with his own determination to attain his unmatched goal of attaining a position superior to Brahma, Dhruva frankly rejected the sage's well-intended advice.

Clear Communication and Clarifying Intentions

Finally, little Dhruva began replying. Thus far, he had silently heard the advice of Narada Muni but denied them mentally. He started speaking, 'O great sage, you have kindly taught me how to attain peace of mind when one's heart is disturbed by happiness and distress. It is certainly a very good instruction. But as far as I am concerned, this kind of philosophy does not touch my heart. Therefore, I cannot accept your instructions. But this impudence is not my fault. Being born in a kshatriya family, I am unable to follow your pieces of advice on peace and internal reconciliation while dealing with situations of life in a philosophically ideal manner.'

The instructions of a wise sage are greatly valued and accepted by people in general with great eagerness and respect. In fact, it is a great fortune to get personal guidance from a great sage like Narada Muni. But here was a young prince who rebuffed the wise words claiming that they didn't suit his kind.

> *Honestly expressing one's inability to follow a superior's advice is not a sin but diplomatically manoeuvring them to say what we want to hear is inappropriate.*

The teachings of tolerance and forgiveness better suit the *brahmanas*. But a kshatriya tormented by harsh words would rather retaliate than tolerate. So, naturally, Dhruva couldn't digest Narada's teachings at this stage.

Although what prince Dhruva did may not be the best way to respond to the excellent advice of a great sage, his honesty must be appreciated. He wholeheartedly appreciated Narada Muni's instructions while honestly expressing his inability to follow them. He wasn't diplomatic but respectful to the sage and also acknowledged his greatness.

Narada Muni didn't take offence to Dhruva's denial. He could empathize with the child's emotions and allowed the boy to express himself openly without obstructing the flow of his emotions. He didn't suppress Dhruva's expressions, which Suruchi had done earlier.

Real empathy flows when we step into the shoes of the one we are dealing with. Switching angles of vision with someone on the other side makes us more sensitive to their situation. As a result, we can speak some benefitting words instead of those hurting their hearts. Such warmth-filled dealings nourish relationships.

If we allow younger ones to open up and pour their hearts out to us instead of suppressing them with prejudice, we can help them better.

Dhruva soberly clarified his intentions to Narada Muni and explained his situation, 'O learned brahmana sage, my stepmother, Suruchi, has lanced my heart with her harsh words. Now my heart is longing to occupy a position more exalted than anyone within the three worlds. I cannot compromise this ambition. This is the goal of my life. If you oblige, kindly advise me on an honest path to achieve my goal.'

Transparently clarifying one's intentions instead of concealing them helps builds good relationships. Thus, clear communication of one's intentions is of vital importance.

While honesty and straightforwardness sustain relationships, diplomacy and hypocrisy strain them.

Apart from denying Narada Muni's advice, Dhruva confidently asked him for a favour that he particularly wanted. He even mentioned Narada's ability to grant such a favour. He said, 'Dear sage, you are a worthy son of Lord Brahma. You travel, playing your musical instrument, the veena, all over the universe, to benefit common people like me. You can show me the way to fulfil my ambition. Please instruct me in this regard.'

Although Dhruva's honesty was worthy of appreciation, his motives were clearly material and selfish—he was overly ambitious and revengeful. Being a pure devotee of Lord Vishnu, how could Narada Muni endorse and support the mentality of worshipping Lord Vishnu for fulfilling selfish ambitions? Do the scriptures not repeatedly injunct that one has to worship the Lord selflessly, without material motives?

What would Narada do now? Would he deny assisting Dhruva in his selfish pursuit? Or would he show the boy the path to achieving what he wanted? Read on to find out.

* * *

Pearls of Wisdom

Relationship Sutras

1. Avoid prejudice and adopt empathy while hearing someone's problem—it is half the solution.
2. Clarifying one's intentions instead of concealing them in the name of modesty makes clear communication.
3. We all are like strangers assembled at a restaurant. Why strain relations for such a short time?
4. Dualities won't affect us the moment we understand our dual identities (body and soul).
5. Pure intentions and honest expressions maintain sanctity in relations, while hypocrisy strains them.

Success Sutras

1. It's not worth being impulsive or getting unduly affected by difficulties. Let's seek the solution that lies beyond lamentation.
2. An unshakable resolve despite reversals and tests is a time-tested formula for success.
3. It's wise to learn from those relatively more successful than you instead of being envious.
4. It's worth befriending someone who is equally successful instead of competing.
5. It's sensible to guide someone who is not as successful as you instead of being oppressive.

4

'Real'izing Ambitions

Determination coupled with mature guidance of experienced well-wishers leads to true success.

'Alright, my dear boy, I shall present to you the way treading which you will be able to fulfil your ambition!' Narada Muni affectionately spoke to Dhruva.

Being a mere child, Dhruva's honesty was not unwelcomed by Narada Muni. Although still a little prince, Dhruva was a kshatriya, so his resolve was not something that startled the sage. Holy texts behest that one must worship Lord Vishnu without any material agendas. But Dhruva desired to outclass every living entity in the universe in terms of wealth and position. He was also revengeful towards his stepmother and stepbrother. All of this, in one sense, maybe he ascribed to his innocence and tender age. But more than all of this, Dhruva's determination to worship Lord Vishnu impressed Narada Muni. Resultantly, he overlooked the boy's motives and instead of taking offence to Dhruva's refusal of his advice, Narada compassionately considered how he could benefit Dhruva by bellowing the fire of resolve within him.

> *To compassionate devotees, the welfare of people in general, is of greater importance than their personal esteem.*

After having tested Dhruva's waters and being reassured of the boy's unflinching determination towards the worship of Lord Vishnu, the sage accepted the boy as his dear disciple. Narada's expertise in inspiring and teaching bhakti to everyone, young and old, is a beautiful feature of his personality.

The Beauty of the Lord's Form

Narada Muni continued, 'Dear child, worshiping Lord Vishnu according to your mother's advice is the best way to attain your goal. Anyone who desires success in one's endeavours must worship the feet of Lord Vishnu and meditate on Him. I wish all good fortune unto you. Now, I shall instruct you how you can fulfil your ambition.'

> *A bona fide guru directs one's disciples to the shelter of the Lord and systematically teaches the method of doing so.*

Dhruva carefully listened to the instructions of Narada Muni. He was well aware of the potency of the great sage.

'My dear Dhruva,' said Narada Muni, 'Now you must go to the bank of river Yamuna where the beautiful forest of Madhuvana is located. I think it would be the right place for you to commence worship, since Lord Krishna eternally resides there. Thus, one who goes there, automatically moves closer to the Lord. First, you must bathe in the sacred waters of River Yamuna three times a day. Then while sitting on an asana in a calm and quiet position, you must practice breath and mind control. Gradually, begin meditating on the divine form of Lord Vishnu. Such meditation is called *dhyana*, which invokes the Lord's blessings profusely on the sincere meditator.'

Only a spiritually elevated guru can describe the characteristics of God and enlighten spiritual seekers.

Narada then described the divine form of Lord Vishnu, which was Dhruva's focus of meditation. 'The Lord's face is extremely beautiful and pleasing. He is always youthful and unaffected by old age, unlike ordinary humans. Every limb of His body is properly formed. His lotus-like eyes, eyebrows, raised nose and broad forehead are extremely charming. His splendour overshadows even the magnificent heavenly devatas. With eyes and lips pink like the rising sun, He wears the *Srivatsa* mark on His chest. His bodily hue is a deep blue. The flower garland around His neck is eternally fresh and unfading. He has four hands that bear a conch shell, a wheel (chakra), a club (*gada*) and a lotus flower. A jewelled crown, dazzling necklaces, bracelets and the unparalleled Kaustubha jewel adorn His neck. He wears yellow silken garments, tiny golden waist bells and ankle bells that decorate His lotus feet. Countless yogis meditate upon this divine form within their hearts which are thus illuminated by the glittering jewel-like toenails of the Lord. Anyone fortunate enough to envision His form or meditate upon it experiences complete satisfaction of the eyes and heart.'

> *Material beauty agitates the mind while spiritual beauty satisfies the mind.*

The Glory of the Lord's Character

Having described the beauty of the Lord's form, Narada Muni began describing the beauty of His character, 'The Lord is the worthiest shelter of all surrendered devotees, for He is an ocean of compassion. He is especially affectionate towards all His devotees. His loving smiles and merciful glances nourish the hearts of all His devotees. Therefore, a devotee should constantly see His form within the heart and expose oneself to His merciful glances. One who meditates in this way is very soon freed from all shortcomings and attains the fulfilment of one's desires.'

> *The beautiful form of a person inspires attraction but, in truth, attachment and affection towards them are actually produced as a result of their beautiful character. Therefore, the enchanting beauty of the*

Lord's form and character is the source of relish and refuge for all.

Dhruva carefully heard Narada Muni speak as he described Lord Vishnu's form. Now, he had to meditate upon that divine form. Dhruva had never heard of such a captivating description of the Lord's form and character. All he had known from his mother about Lord Vishnu was that He fulfils the worshipper's desires. But now, he was getting to know the Lord's personality and qualities in great detail.

Yet, Dhruva wasn't ready to fall in love with the Lord but considered Him only as a means to attain his goals. Many people perceive the Lord as a desire-fulfiller, or in other words, an order supplier, and at that point, Dhruva was a part of this class of worshippers. Although Narada Muni was cognizant of this, he still was personally guiding Dhruva in his meditation on Lord Vishnu. Narada Muni was inspiring the boy to become a sincere devotee, for he knew that in the time to come, the ambitious child would be filtered of all his impure motives, impulsive nature and greed for the position as a result of his meditation on Lord Vishnu.

Maturity of God's realization is when we go beyond seeing Him just as a desire-fulfiller to seeing Him as a loving reciprocator.

The Power of Mantra Meditation

Later, Narada Muni taught a special mantra to Dhruva that he would need to chant while meditating as instructed.

Revealing the mantra to Dhruva, Narada Muni spoke, 'My dear child, please chant this twelve-syllable mantra for worshiping Lord Krishna: "*Om namo bhagavate vasudevaya*".'

The Lord has unlimited names and forms. Unlike the names of people in this world that often do not match their qualities, all the names of the Lord fully reflect His characteristics and activities. For instance, He is called 'Vishnu' because He is all-pervading. He is known as 'Krishna' because He is all-attractive. He is also known as 'Vasudeva' because He is understood on the spiritual platform. He is also called 'Govinda' because He gives pleasure to the cows. By sincerely and repeatedly chanting any of the divine names of the Lord, one connects one's heart with Him, develops a love for Him and invokes His all-auspicious presence.

Chanting the names of God is the best means to establish a connection between our hearts and His grace.

The Power of Worship

Narada Muni further instructed Dhruva, 'Apart from meditating on the Lord's form and chanting this mantra, you can also make a physical form of the Lord with clay. Such a deity is non-different from the Lord. Offer Him flowers, fruits, water and whatever is available in the forest. Tulasi leaves are especially dear to the Lord and grow profusely in Vrindavan. So please offer abundant Tulasi to Him.'

As Dhruva attentively learned from his guru, the process of meditation on the Lord's form, chanting the twelve-syllable mantra and worshipping His deity, Narada Muni concluded, 'Dear Dhruva, you must also meditate upon the transcendental activities of Lord Vishnu in His different incarnations.'

The process seemed to be rigorous and time-consuming. Was it really practical for a five-year-old?—Yes! With determination and one-pointed attention, anything is possible. The intricate process of worship and meditation taught by Narada Muni didn't put Dhruva off. Instead, he was fully committed to following the path with all sincerity and had fixed his gaze on his goal. There was no question of turning back. Dhruva bowed down at Narada Muni's feet and circumambulated the sage, his guru. Then, he started for Madhuvana, the forest that is always imprinted with the lotus footprints of Lord Krishna.

Thus, Narada Muni gently and intelligently directed Dhruva and dovetailed his determination in devotion unto Lord Vishnu. Whatever Narada Muni's acts may appear to be, his mission has always been to connect people from diverse backgrounds to God. Narada Muni had mentored another child disciple, Prahlada, born in a family of demons. Narada inspired devotion in Prahlada's heart even when he was within the womb of his mother. Eventually, Prahlada became an illustrious devotee of Lord Vishnu. Narada Muni also converted a cruel hunter named Mrigari into a gentle devotee of Lord Krishna, by teaching him this system of impactful mantra meditation.

Kind-hearted people like Narada Muni cannot see common people being misguided or confused. So, they do their best to elevate others.

Having thus inspired Dhruva, Narada Muni considered visiting Dhruva's father, Uttanapada, at his palace. He wanted to meet the king and understand his situation after his son had left the palace. How did Uttanapada react to Dhruva's sudden departure from his palace? What would Narada Muni speak to him? Would he admonish the king for his misbehaviour towards Dhruva? Flip the page to uncover the answers to these questions.

* * *

Pearls of Wisdom

Relationship Sutras

1. Prioritize the welfare of your dependents over your personal esteem.
2. Go beyond seeing God as a desire-fulfiller to seeing Him as a loving reciprocator.
3. A compassionate heart keeps aside the cushion of comfort to serve others selflessly.

Success Sutras

1. Focus on a character that inspires people's hearts rather than accomplishments that impress their minds.

5

Comforting a Repentant Heart

To the extent, one values a relation with someone, to that extent, one becomes genuinely regretful of one's mistakes in that relationship.

'I've acted like a henpecked husband. Being addicted to sensory enjoyment, I behaved insensitively. Oh, what a stony-hearted person I have been! All condemnation upon me!'

King Uttanapada's regret knew no bounds. He was remorseful for having been a husband dominated by one of his wives and an irresponsible father. Sitting morosely in his magnificent palace, his mind kept running towards his son, Dhruva. In the absence of Dhruva, his opulence, power, influence, servants, treasury and royal paraphernalia gave him no satisfaction. This was because he was concerned about the well-being and whereabouts of Dhruva.

Irreversible Mistakes

Uttanapada was certainly a great soul. He was also a devotee of Lord Vishnu. But somehow, he became overly attached to his younger wife and couldn't treat his elder wife and her son properly. He did not welcome little Dhruva when he tried to sit on his lap.

It was not that Uttanapada housed no affection for Dhruva. On the contrary, he certainly loved his son. But his disproportionate attachment towards Suruchi prohibited him from welcoming Dhruva and forbidding Suruchi from insulting him. In this way, the king had surely erred. However, in time, he realized that the situation had already slipped out of his hands and his son had left his palace, broken-hearted.

Some errors are irremediable. We can't always mend things.

Sometimes, even though we realize our mistakes and try to rectify them, the opportunity to seek forgiveness may have already walked past us. At times, we may correct our mistakes and avoid their reactions. But sometimes, we have to accept the consequences of those errors inevitably. For instance, after coming out of the examination hall, a student cannot modify his answer sheet even if he realizes that he has used the wrong formula to solve a mathematical problem. Similarly, if a cook realizes that the salt he has added to a dish exceeds what is required, he cannot undo it.

Time wasted and words spoken are like arrows that have left the bow—they cannot be retracted.

Therefore, we should learn to act appropriately. But the good news is that there is a glimmer of hope.

A Ray of Hope

Firstly, we must be careful not to make mistakes, but, as they say, to err is human. Even great souls like Uttanapada made mistakes. That does not mean the end of the world. It isn't a mistake to make a mistake, but it's a mistake to intentionally repeat the same mistake. After all, we learn not just from our success but from our failures!

One can learn from one's mistakes and be cautious not to repeat them in future. Having failed in one exam, a student ramps up his preparation for the following examination. A distasteful dish can be made up for by cooking a delicious preparation next time. There is always scope for improvement.

Accepting failures in the right spirit paves the way for future success.

An honest person regrets having said or done something that hurt someone in any way. His or her future good behaviour is born out of such honest regret. Uttanapada truly repented for his wrongdoing—spending his time in self-condemnation, he appeared dull and pale. Being the son of the most celebrated Svayambhuva Manu and the grandson of Lord Brahma, such mistreatment of his child and wife wasn't expected of Uttanapada. But as a genuine person, he was ashamed of his act and was immersed in self-reproach.

> *It's best to act appropriately in a situation rather than regret it later. It's better to regret one's poor behaviour rather than justify it. It's worse to justify one's impulsive act and disown all responsibility for its result!*

Empathize, Don't Pressurize!

As Uttanapada sulked gloomily in the inner chambers of his palace, Narada Muni arrived. The king immediately stood up, respectfully welcomed the great sage and offered him an elevated seat. He washed Narada Muni's feet humbly and stood silently.

Pleased with the king's hospitality yet concerned about his predicament, Narada Muni asked Uttanapada, 'My dear King, is everything well with you? You don't seem to be very happy and your face appears withered. It seems that you have been thinking of something deeply for a long time. What has happened? I hope your duties of managing the state and protecting the citizens are going well, and you are enjoying your royal position with full prosperity.'

Indeed, Narada Muni was well aware of Uttanapada's condition at that moment. Yet, he inquired from Uttanapada in this way only to induce the King into personally revealing his mind before the great sage. Narada Muni didn't immediately admonish the king for his past misbehaviour or bombard him with his instructions or solutions. Instead, he gave the king space so he could fully express his emotions.

Allowing others to express their emotions and empathetically hearing them speak has a calming effect on their minds.

Sometimes people understand their mistakes even before we point them out. Therefore, instead of being too eager to correct others, we must allow them to realize their shortcomings while being ready to assist them appropriately.

Our offer of help to others shouldn't spark the mood of superiority in us—instead, it must spawn the mood of service.

Rectify, Don't Justify!

Uttanapada replied to Narada Muni, 'O best of the brahmanas, I am very sinful. I had become excessively addicted to my younger wife, Suruchi, and abandoned my noble wife, Suniti, and her five-year-old son, Dhruva. I practically banished both of them with my neglectful and insensitive behaviour. As a henpecked husband, I lost all my intelligence, common sense and kindness. Moreover, I have mistreated my son.' Narada Muni patiently listened.

Anxious about his son, Uttanapada continued, 'The face of my son is just like a tender lotus flower. I'm very worried about his precarious condition. He left my palace without informing anyone. I do not know his whereabouts. He is unprotected and might be very hungry. He must be lying down somewhere in the forest and the wolves, lions or tigers may have attacked him and mauled his tender body.' Uttanapada's emotions choked him up while he poured out his heart to Narada Muni.

A prudent heart regrets genuinely when it fails to respond sensitively. Honest repentance for one's misdeeds appears in the heart of a noble person.

Uttanapada piteously lamented the safety of his son. His regret had struck his heart with grief. He continued to criticize himself, 'Alas, just see how I was conquered by my own attraction to my younger wife. I have become so cruel. Out of love and affection, the little child was trying to get on my lap, but I did not have the heart to receive him. Nor did I pat him even for one moment. I have become so hard-hearted and vile.'

A mistake is a mistake if one fails to learn from it. Honest regret, sincere apology, the effort to improve, and endeavour not to repeat—make one perfect soon.'

Reassurance for Sincere Repentance

Uttanapada was in no mood to justify his misdeed, instead, he felt genuine guilt and remorse. Seeing him aggrieved, Narada Muni consoled and encouraged him.

'My dear King, please do not worry about your son. He will be well protected by the Supreme Lord Vishnu. Although you have no information about his glory, he is extremely competent. His reputation will be spread all over the world. He will perform activities that even great sages and kings would find impossible. At present, he is absorbed in worshiping the Lord in Madhuvana. Soon, he will complete his austerities and become successful in his mission. Then, he will surely return and give you happiness. You will be able to see him and bathe him in your love and affection. He will enhance your reputation all over the world and in the future, you will be famous as the father of glorious Dhruva.'

With these encouraging words, Narada Muni reassured the king. Uttanapada felt hopeful and was extremely grateful to Narada Muni. Thereafter, Narada Muni departed from the king's palace.

Thenceforth, Uttanapada practically gave up all his kingly duties and simply began to think of his son Dhruva. His interest in his vast and opulent kingdom faded away.

The intelligence that identifies one's own faults is wonderful, the heart that repents for them is glorious and the conscience that endeavours not to repeat them is admirable.

Resultantly, Uttanapada treated Suniti lovingly and desperately waited for his son's arrival. Gradually, Suruchi's heart was also transformed and she gave up her inimical attitude towards Suniti.

But what happened to Dhruva? Was he safe at Madhuvana? Could he follow the instructions of Narada Muni? Would he find success in his mission of pleasing Lord Vishnu and thereby attain boons from Him? That only the next chapter can reveal.

* * *

Pearls of Wisdom

Relationship Sutras

1. Don't be too eager to point out other's flaws, give them space to realize on their own.
2. Help others not in the mood of superiority but in the mood of service.

Success Sutras

1. Accept failures in the right spirit.
2. Rectify your mistakes, don't justify them.
3. Regret your mistakes, don't repeat them.
4. Repentance does not amount to dysfunctionality.
5. Some errors may not be reversible but can be repairable.
6. The mind makes us deliberately commit downtrodden acts and then fools us by claiming it to be a mistake.
7. While hoping for the best, we shouldn't put our hands to rest.

6

Success in Six Months

The trio for success – 1. Desire, 2. Endeavour and 3. Prayer One's 'desire' must be pure and strong, one's 'endeavour' has to be sincere and determined, yet without the Lord's sanction, one can't be successful, therefore, 'prayer' is necessary.

After being instructed by his mentor in the process of worshipping Lord Vishnu, Dhruva went to Madhuvana. Arriving at the bank of the Yamuna, he entered the river to take a bath. Later that night, he diligently observed a fast.

Then, as advised by Narada Muni, he began his worship of the Lord in the beautiful forest of Madhuvana. Dhruva's austerities in the forest set a great example for all seekers for eons to come. The level of his determination and the intensity of his resolve was unparalleled even as a five-year-old child.

Increasing Intensity of Austerities

Dhruva began worshipping Lord Vishnu sincerely and restricted his eating only to fruits and berries named Kapittha and Badara, only once in three days, to keep his body alive. In this way, he spent one full month.

In the second month, Dhruva survived on some dry grass and leaves that he took only once in six days. Without wasting even a moment searching for food or other things, Dhruva became absorbed in his worship of the Lord.

During the third month, Dhruva's austerities and his absorption in Lord Vishnu increased. He simply drank water only once every nine days. Thus, he remained rapt in meditation and eventually entered a trance while worshipping the Lord.

As the fourth month set in, Dhruva's sadhana spiritual practice intensified further. He mastered *pranayama* or breathing exercises, and would inhale air only once in twelve days. Being completely fixed up in his position as a devotee of Lord Vishnu, he took only air as his food.

By the fifth month, Dhruva's meditation reached its crescendo. He had completely controlled his breathing, attained perfection in the process and was able to stand simply on one leg. Like a motionless column, Dhruva fully concentrated on the form of Lord Vishnu in line with the teachings of his guru, Narada Muni. He continually chanted and meditated on the mantra 'om namo bhagavate vasudevaya.'

The power of sincere meditation on the divine form of the Lord makes one completely absorbed in a trance.

Complete Self-control

Dhruva attained complete sense control. His senses were not at all agitated by any sense object. Generally, the greatest obstacle in spiritual life or even in one's normal life is the distraction caused by the senses—our eyes constantly chase beautiful objects, our ears long to hear pleasant sounds and music, our hands hanker to touch soft objects that give pleasure to the body, our nose continually pursues sweet fragrances, and the tongue wishes to taste palatable dishes even if they may hamper one's health. In this way, an average human being is constantly tormented by sensual attractions that are nothing but distractions. But Dhruva's senses were riveted on his goal—worshipping Lord Vishnu.

Another great obstacle for a person engaged in spiritual practices is mental distractions. In fact, the senses become distracted because of a distracted mind. Whenever the senses come in contact with sense objects, they create various pleasant and unpleasant impressions within the mind. For instance, when a person sees a beautiful object, a pleasant impression is immediately created in the mind and when the same person sees an ugly object, an unpleasant impression is generated in the mind.

Thus, the mind becomes a storehouse of millions and trillions of material impressions that keep popping up regularly and distract the person from his or her goals. Therefore, mind and sense control are vital to attaining success in any endeavour, especially in spiritual life.

One who can control one's mind and senses is a deserving candidate and becomes entitled to success.

Although immature in age, Dhruva exhibited complete sense and mind control in his devotional meditation on Lord Vishnu. He was also fully determined to follow the path instructed by his guru.

A student who is sincere in following the instructions of a potent guru is sure to attain success in spiritual life.

The Lord in the Heart

Dhruva's determined practice of meditating on the Lord brought him to a stage where he experienced a complete trance. He could totally absorb himself in the form of Lord Vishnu and eventually captivate the Lord within his heart.

The Lord likes to be arrested within the loving hearts of His devotees.

Although Dhruva's meditation was materially motivated, he did not meditate on his material ambition while following the process taught by Narada Muni. Rather, he was fixed on his meditation on the Lord. Thus, Dhruva was purified of his selfish desires and the Lord was captured in his uncontaminated heart.

Sincere worship of the Lord purifies one of all ill motives.

Just like we desire to stay in a clean place devoid of dirt, similarly, the Lord prefers to reside in a clean heart devoid of greed, envy, and pride.

The Lord, the master of the entire universe, who holds it within His belly, was now captured within the home of Dhruva's heart. At the dawn of creation, Lord Vishnu was lying on the ocean while a lotus sprouted from His navel. That lotus grew bigger and bigger, and Lord Brahma was born within that gigantic lotus. Thus, Lord Vishnu is the father of Lord Brahma. Vishnu is the primary creator of the entire universe, while Brahma, His son, is a secondary creator.

Within the lotus on which Lord Brahma was seated were the fourteen planetary systems inhabited by living beings of different natures. As human beings, we are currently situated on the earthly plane (*Bhu-loka*). Above the earthly plane is the heavenly plane (*Bhuvar-loka* and *Svarga-loka*), where the devatas or the gods who control the various affairs of the universe reside. And above the heavenly plane are several other planes (*Jana-loka, Mahar-loka, Tapo-loka* and *Satya-loka*) in which perfected beings, great sages and Lord Brahma resides. Below the earthly plane are seven planes (*Atala, Vitala,*

Sutala, Talatala, Mahatala, Rasatala and *Patalalokas*) inhabited by various living beings, including snakes and others.

This entire universe exists within the belly of Lord Vishnu and comes out from His abdomen at the beginning of creation. All the planets within the universe are manifested at the start of the day of Brahma. At the end of Brahma's day, they return to Lord Vishnu's body and re-manifest at the beginning of the next day of Brahma. Thus, Lord Vishnu is the Supreme Father and Mother of the entire universe, carrying it within Himself.

As Heavy as the Universe

The Lord, the master of the entire universe, who holds it within His belly, was now under the custody of Dhruva's heart. Thus, the universe was also entrapped within Dhruva. Little Dhruva thus assumed the entire weight of the universe by carrying the Lord within Himself.

As Dhruva steadied himself on one leg, the pressure of his tender toe pushed the earth down. Just like an elephant being carried within a boat rocks the boat left and right with its every step—similarly, little Dhruva, who was carrying the Lord within his heart, started shaking the boat of the planet Earth. The entire earth started quivering and that alarmed the devatas.

This feat of Dhruva seemed unthinkable. However, it is not very difficult to understand this happening with an example. Hundreds of people sit in an airplane that travels at a speed of thousands of kilometres per hour.

Although every individual in the airplane has limited body weight and a unique pace at which he or she walks or runs, still, because they are all seated in the airplane, they move at the speed of thousands of kilometres an hour as well. Individually, they cannot move at such great speed. But having taken shelter within the airplane, they're now able to move. Similarly, in his own capacity, Dhruva was just a five-year-old child who did not weigh much. But no sooner did he take shelter of the Lord than his weight equalled that of the Lord.

If a person becomes a pure devotee and elevates oneself in spiritual consciousness, such a person can change the world's total consciousness into God's consciousness. Spiritual bliss is too contagious to be contained.

Thus, Dhruva pushed down the Earth with his toe unknowingly. As a part of his yoga practice, he closed all the holes in his body and consequently, the universe within his body became choked up. As a result, all the living beings within the universe felt suffocated. Each living entity in the universe began gasping for air.

Prayers of Supplication in Suffocation

Suffocated, all the devatas approached the Supreme Lord Vishnu for help and prayed, 'O Lord, You are the shelter of all moving and non-moving living beings in the entire universe. At this moment, the respiration of all living entities is getting hampered. We have never experienced such a thing before. You are the only refuge we all have. Kindly save us from this catastrophe. We cannot comprehend why this unusual phenomenon has come before us.'

When the devatas thus intensely prayed for help, Lord Vishnu said, 'Dear devatas, do not get perturbed by this. This is the effect of the severe and determined *tapasya* of my young devotee, Dhruva. Now he is fully absorbed in meditating on Me. Thus, he has obstructed the universal breathing unknowingly. You can safely return to your homes. I shall go to the boy immediately and you will surely be saved from this situation. Do not fear.'

When Lord Vishnu thus reassured the devatas, their fears soon vanished. They offered obeisances unto the Lord and returned to their heavenly planets.

An Unparalleled Accomplishment

At Madhuvana, Dhruva experienced something supernatural. In the maturity of his yogic meditation, he could see the brilliant form of Lord Vishnu within his heart and thus experience spiritual bliss through Lord Vishnu's *darshan* (vision).

Collecting that divine form within his heart is something marvellous that Dhruva achieved only within six months of tapasya. Great sages and yogis take millions of years to be qualified to see the Lord within their hearts through meditation. But here, Dhruva accomplished this inconceivable goal within a short span of six months, at the age of five.

Age, caste, gender, nationality, wealth, education and so on are neither disqualifications nor qualifications to please the Lord. He is impressed only with sincere devotion.

The Secret of Success

The example of Dhruva clearly shows that it doesn't take millions of lifetimes to attain the Lord's favour. It only takes some moments of sincere devotion and alignment to the instructions of a bona fide guru. To the level we are aligned with the instructions of the guru to that degree, we will be able to attain the mercy of the Lord. Therefore, taking inspiration from Dhruva's life, we should also perform our spiritual practices under the guidance of seniors. As a sincere disciple, Dhruva aligned himself with the instructions of Narada Muni, his guru, and performed bhakti with full determination, without any deviation, and achieved success within six months.

Sincerely following the guidelines of spiritual mentors with determination in spiritual practices makes the Lord reciprocate.

But suddenly, Dhruva lost that vision of the Lord within his heart. Would he be able to see the Lord again? Would the Lord fulfil the ambitious desires of Dhruva? Well, getting to the answers would take a turn of the page.

* * *

Pearls of Wisdom

Relationship Sutras

1. A heart that's devoid of ill motives and filled with pure intentions can relish the juice in relationships.
2. Our heart is too tiny to accommodate all sorts of dirt and the Divine at the same time. Let's cleanse the heart from the dirt of greed, envy and pride.
3. Modern age austerity is to stop gossiping and start speaking for others' benefit.

Success Sutras

1. Control the fickle mind and sense like a tortoise withdrawing its limbs from all sorts of danger.
2. Stop worrying about useless thoughts and start pulling your mind away from them. It's difficult but not impossible if we are determined!
3. Seek a reliable guru intelligently and follow his teachings diligently.
4. Don't ignore the instructions of a guru who can remove the ignorance in the heart.

7

Transformation by Divine Touch

One who experiences the bliss of God's love doesn't hanker for temporary positions and possessions in this world. To attain such devotion and detachment is a spiritual success.

Dhruva was perturbed. After having blissfully envisioned the Lord within his heart, the Lord's beautiful form suddenly vanished and left little Dhruva anxious. Disappointment blanketed him and his meditation was intercepted. But the loss of this wonderful vision was compensated by a rare fortune that generally demands ages of practice and patience.

Lord Vishnu was keen to meet His young devotee Dhruva. The Lord summoned His bird carrier, the mighty Garuda and immediately headed to the forest of Madhuvana, where Dhruva, His young devotee, had absorbed himself in a devotional trance. The Lord is compassionate and merciful to any devotee who worships Him with unflagging determination and loving devotion. To the Lord, it is immaterial whether the devotee is a child or a grown-up, a man or a woman, an Indian or an American.

When we fervently worship the Lord, the Lord becomes eager to see us.

Disappointment That Turned into Excitement

With his meditation now deterred, he gradually opened his eyes, leaving his state of trance. To his surprise, before his eyes was the same Lord Vishnu whom he had envisioned within his heart! Dhruva was stunned. Overwhelmed with astonishment, jubilation and excitement, Dhruva became bewildered. Then, spontaneously, he fell flat like a rod at Lord Vishnu's divine feet.

Sincere meditation on the Lord leads to a direct vision of the Lord. Such a visualization overwhelms a devotee with spiritual bliss and satisfaction.

The Lord showered His affectionate glances upon the child who had now transformed into an exalted devotee. With his emotions streaming forth, Dhruva beheld Lord Vishnu as if he were drinking the Lord with his eyes, kissing His feet with his mouth and embracing Him with his arms. Horripilation due to unparalleled spiritual bliss covered Dhruva's body with the goosebumps of ecstasy.

The sublimity of this experience was overwhelming and Dhruva thus stood before the Lord with folded hands.

Equipped with Knowledge

Although he was a mere child, Dhruva desired to praise the Lord with suitable words. As an inexperienced child, upon seeing the Lord, he did not have the necessary knowledge, vocabulary or poetic ability to praise the Lord appropriately as many great sages, devatas and devotees had done before.

Lord Vishnu understood Dhruva's awkward situation and felt compassion for him. Out of His kindness, the Lord touched His divine, spotless, white conch shell to the forehead of little Dhruva. The Lord's conch shell, named *Panchajanya*, is non-different from the Vedas. As soon as the Panchajanya touched Dhruva's forehead, he felt the essence of all Vedic knowledge instantly reveal within his heart. Dhruva became spontaneously enlightened with the conclusions and details of all Vedic scriptures.

Imbued with deep knowledge, wisdom and realization of the Lord as well as all spiritual subject matters, Dhruva's heart had been instantaneously transfigured. At the age of five, within six months of meditating on Lord Vishnu, Dhruva attained the position of a pure devotee. He was endowed with realized spiritual wisdom. Dhruva's unparalleled success is celebrated throughout the universe, even today.

Extraordinary knowledge and renunciation are return gifts for those who practice devotion incessantly.

Being fully cognizant of all Vedic conclusions and spiritual truths, the young devotee Dhruva started offering beautiful prayers to Lord Vishnu.

The inspiration and ability in us even to offer prayers to the Lord come from the Lord.

All one needs is a sincere desire to serve the Lord. The Lord then mercifully reciprocates and empowers the devotee to do so.

Our Praise Is by His Grace

Dhruva began speaking. 'My dear Lord, You are all-powerful. You have entered within me and have enlivened all my dormant senses—my hands, legs, ears, touch sensation and especially my power of speech. I am able to speak and praise you only because of the inspiration and empowerment you have given me.'

But what did Dhruva mean when he said the Lord had awakened his sleeping senses? During the past six months, Dhruva had tirelessly and sleeplessly performed austerities to attain the Lord's blessings. Why then, did Dhruva say that his senses had been sleeping thus far and that the Lord had enlivened them?! This is because Dhruva had realized that the senses are as good as sleeping until they're utilized in the Lord's service.

As long as the senses are acting on a material plane for material purposes and are not engaged in spiritual activities, they are said to be sleeping.

Now that Dhruva had realized the importance of spiritual life and felt satisfied at heart, having personally seen the Lord, he understood deeper spiritual truths. He understood the right utilization of one's senses—in the Lord's service. Our hands, legs, ears, tongue, mind and everything are meant for the Lord's service. After all, we are all his children, aren't we?

Dhruva continued to pray, 'O Lord, You are the Supreme Personality who manifests the entire material creation with Your divine energy. You are the source and sustenance of the universe. Without you being its foundation, the creation has no existence. Even my great grandfather Brahma is fully surrendered unto You. Right in the beginning of the creation, You enlightened Brahma with the knowledge of the Vedas. By Your empowerment, he could assist You in creating all the planets and bodies of living beings within this universe. O Lord, You are the friend of the distressed. One who has perfect knowledge loves You, and serves You selflessly.'

What about His Ambition?

Thus, Dhruva fervently described the Lord's divine characteristics in his prayers. What would he do next? Would he ask the Lord to fulfil his wishes, for which he had performed six months of austerity? Was he still angry with his stepmother, jealous of his stepbrother and desirous of great position and wealth?

No! Dhruva had been fully transmuted. He no longer had material motives or selfish desires. By dint of his sincere worship and devotional mediation, he got the darshan of the Lord personally and soon forgot his original desire. He became so immersed in bhakti that he had been remodelled along with his material objective.

Unsurprisingly, Dhruva began criticizing the desire to possess any material position in this world. He said, 'O Lord, some people worship You simply for their sense enjoyment, under the spell of illusion. You are like a desire tree and can fulfil the desire of any person who approaches You. However, foolish people desire perishable material boons which only offer temporary happiness. Although you can bestow liberation from the repeated cycle of birth and death in this world, and put a complete full stop to all material miseries, still people request material prosperity from You!'

With a heart fully satisfied with devotion and a mature realization of the Lord's affection, Dhruva condemned the mentality of the aspirations for unworthy material boons that he had housed in his heart earlier.

The glaring jewels of wealth, beauty and fame in this world blind us with attachment and ego, but the brilliance of the real jewel of devotion to God enlivens us with unending satisfaction.

The Bliss of Devotion

The perennial channel of devotion and ecstatic emotion in Dhruva continued to flow. 'My dear Lord,' said Dhruva, 'The divine bliss derived from meditating upon You and hearing about Your qualities and activities from Your devotees is unlimited. The happiness of attaining heaven is insignificant compared to that spiritual bliss. Even if one is elevated to the heaven by amassing countless credits having performed pious activities (*punya*), one has to fall from heaven to this earth after those credits are exhausted. No one can eternally reside in heaven because heaven itself is a material planet and is subject to annihilation one day. But one who selflessly worships and serves You can attain eternal life in Your spiritual abode *Vaikuntha*, reaching which one need not come back to this temporary world of miseries.'

How, then can one attain Vaikuntha? How can one achieve eternal life—the ultimate success of human life? In his mature realization, Dhruva progressively describes the process of acquiring an eternal life of spiritual bliss. In fact, by following this process, one can create Vaikuntha anywhere one is present.

Dhruva continued. 'O Lord, manifesting Vaikuntha here is only possible in the association of great devotees who love You as their heart and soul. In the company of such great devotees, a river of spiritual conversations comes into being. One who is drenched in that nectar-river experiences the immortal spiritual happiness. The company of like-minded devotees inspires devotion within one and all and makes them lovers of Your divine self. Therefore, I prefer the association of such devotees, which leads to eternal life.'

Dhruva had met his guru, Narada Muni and had heard from him the wonderful qualities of Lord Vishnu. Soon,

Dhruva became attracted to the Lord. Before meeting Narada Muni, Dhruva had heard from Suniti that the Lord's affection for His devotee is equivalent to the affection of millions of mothers put together. Dhruva personally experienced that affection in the last six months due to his devotional meditation. Further, Dhruva was enlightened by the touch of the Lord's conch shell. Considering these factors, Dhruva, despite being a child, attained a mature realization of the Lord and the process of bhakti unto Him. He understood that the joy of bhakti is far superior to the temporary joys of the earth and heaven. He could fathom the importance of associating with devotees, enabling one to receive Lord Vishnu's mercy.

Thus, Dhruva shared his heartfelt realizations before the Lord and became oblivious to his previous aspirations. Eventually, Dhruva began concluding his prayers. 'O all-merciful Lord,' he said, 'Those who worship You with devotion, free of all desire, are most fortunate. No boon is as great as the opportunity to serve and worship You and thus become an object of Your mercy. But ignorant people like me worship you with some material objective. You are the merciful maintainer of every devotee. Just like a cow takes care of a newborn calf by supplying milk and protecting it from all attacks, similarly, You maintain, nourish and protect Your devotee in the most appropriate way. I personally do not know what is beneficial for me but You know it beyond doubt, for You are the supreme well-wisher of all.'

Thus, Dhruva offered his prayers unto the Lord. Dhruva had given up all material ambitions and as a result of his own bhakti, his desires and heart were reformed. Now, Lord Vishnu was about to respond to his prayers.

How does Lord Vishnu reply? Does the Lord appreciate Dhruva's sacrifice of his ambition? Would Dhruva receive some special boons from the Lord? Flip forward to find out.

* * *

Pearls of Wisdom

Success Sutras

1. With character and determination in place, age and gender don't even qualify as criteria for success.
2. Unlock the spiritual potency of the material senses.
3. Sow your seeds but pray for the rains.
4. Maintain pure desires and sincere endeavours.
5. Seek what is of true value—wealth, fame, devotion and satisfaction!
6. Don't be overconfident in your power, seek empowerment from the source of all power—God.
7. Do what is humanly possible but it all depends on God's sanction.

8

Ill Motives End Up in Guilt

There is no satisfaction in selfishness. Only selflessness in relationships can satisfy the self and others.

'My dear Dhruva, you are a determined prince. You have executed spiritual practices with great resolve. I know the desire within your heart. Although it is very difficult to fulfil, I shall still grant it. All good fortune unto you.' Lord Vishnu spoke in a grave yet sweet voice in response to the prayers of little Dhruva.

After having nourished his heart for six months with devotional meditation on Lord Vishnu, now Dhruva's heart was completely cleansed of all the envy, revengeful feelings and ambition for position and wealth. Yet, Lord Vishnu noted Dhruva's previous desires. A five-year-old wishing for a position superior to Brahma's was certainly childish, but the Lord nevertheless satisfied the boy's demand out of fatherly affection.

Long-cherished Desire Fulfilled!

The Lord said, 'My dear Dhruva, you desired a position and opulence superior to even Lord Brahma. So, I shall award you, Vaikuntha, the greatest planet, My own abode. That eternal planet of Mine would be famous as *Dhruvaloka* or the Pole Star. Even during the universal dissolution at the end of the millennium, Dhruvaloka will continue to exist. No one has ever ruled that planet. All the planets and stars in the solar system surround Dhruvaloka. All the luminaries in the sky circumambulate it just as bulls tread around a central pole while crushing grains in a traditional mill. Even the *Saptarishi* mandala, or the stars inhabited by the seven great sages, circumambulate Dhruvaloka. This residence is eternal and outshines all the planets (in the zodiac belt), constellations and stars.'

Thus, Lord Vishnu awarded Dhruva His personal abode whose greatness outclasses even Brahmaloka and remains forevermore. The position of Lord Brahma is unequalled within this universe. How can anyone attain a position superior to that? The position greater than that of Brahma is the position of Lord Vishnu Himself, and so is His abode, Vaikuntha. Thus, the Lord granted Vaikuntha to Dhruva.

Sovereignty for 36,000 years

What about Dhruva's innocent desire to sit on his father Uttanapada's lap or throne? What about his revengeful feelings towards his stepmother and stepbrother?—

Lord Vishnu addressed them as well. He said, 'My dear Dhruva, after your father retires and goes to the forest, you will sit on his throne. You will be crowned as king. You will rule the entire world for 36,000 years. All your senses will remain as strong as they are now. You will never become old. I'm bestowing upon you prolonged vigour and longevity.'

The fact that Dhruva would rule the world for 36,000 years is not something startling because, in the *Satya-yuga*, people used to live up to 1,00,000 years. In the *Treta-yuga*, people lived up to 10,000 years. In *Dvapar-yuga*, people had a lifespan of up to 1000 years and in *Kaliyuga*, people live a maximum of up to 100 years. With the change in the yugas, life span, memory, kindness and other good qualities diminish.

Further, the Lord wants mature devotees like Dhruva to rule the earth. Such kings uphold spiritual culture in their kingdoms apart from taking care of their citizens' welfare. Under the rule of such kings, Mother Earth becomes prosperous and citizens live happily in this world while trying to attain a better world in the future.

Penalty for Offence

Lord Vishnu continued, 'Sometime in the future, your brother Uttama will go hunting in the forest and while engrossed in his pursuit, he will be killed by a powerful *Yaksha*. Being dazed upon Uttama's death, Suruchi will also enter the forest searching for her son. While looking for him, she will be devoured by a forest fire. Thus, your stepmother and stepbrother will die.'

Dhruva was displeased with Suruchi's behaviour. He was severely hurt by her sharp, wounding words. But now, Dhruva was no longer an ordinary person, and was now a great devotee of Vishnu. One who insults or offends such a devotee is sure to be punished appropriately. In Mahabharata, Duryodhana and his supporters offended the virtuous Pandavas in several ways and Lord Krishna orchestrated the Kurukshetra war to appropriately punish the evil-minded Duryodhana and others.

The Lord can tolerate offences to Himself but not to His devotees.

In this way, Lord Vishnu personally foretold the resultant consequences of having offended a devotee in the case of Suruchi. We must never insult a devotee or anyone in general. What if they become great devotees like Dhruva? When Suruchi insulted Dhruva, he was just a child. She didn't know Dhruva would grow up to be a great devotee, so her offence was committed unknowingly. Yet she the consequences of her offence waited to embrace her.

The Lord especially favours a devotee. Pleasing or displeasing a devotee directly affects the pleasure or displeasure of the Lord. Therefore, one must be scrupulous in dealings with other devotees and should not unnecessarily offend, insult or hurt them.

Time to Come to Me

Foretelling the future activities of Dhruva, Lord Vishnu continued, 'O Dhruva, you will become the performer of many great sacrifices and the giver of colossal charities. You will be able to enjoy the blessings of all your citizens and lead a very happy life on earth for 36,000 years. Your activities will make you famous. At the time of death, you will be able to remember Me and come to My planet, which the residents of all other planets worship. That planet will be known as Dhruvaloka. Once you arrive there, you will never have to come back to this material world.'

Thus, the Lord gifted Dhruva His own abode. This resulted from Dhruva's sincere tapasya that lasted for six months. After having thus blessed His young devotee Dhruva, Lord Vishnu returned to His abode on the back of Garuda.

Dhruva's success was not ordinary. His accomplishment and good fortune were unparalleled. The boons he received were the apex of rarity and the time he spent to attain such success was only six months. It takes several lifetimes for many stalwart yogis to be able to please the Lord and attain His planet. But Dhruva did that effortlessly—because of his faith in his guru's instructions and his dedication while executing them.

One can become successful in attaining one's goal through expert guidance and determined practice.

Dissatisfaction of the Rare Accomplishment

Dhruva's desire to attain a position superior to Brahma had been fulfilled and his bitter feelings towards his stepmother and stepbrother had fizzled out. His innocent desire to sit on his father's throne has also been fulfilled. Yet, still, there was something that left him unsatisfied! He felt a sense of incompleteness in his heart. Glumly and morosely, he considered himself unfulfilled. Then why did he think so?

Dhruva's heart, pierced by the arrows of Suruchi's harsh words, longed to prove his superiority and made him ambitious. However, his mother told him not to maintain revengeful thoughts toward anyone. She had also asked him to understand that whatever one faces in one's life is only a result of one's previous activities, but Dhruva could not accept that advice. Earlier, when Narada Muni counselled him to give up his ambitious plans, Dhruva rejected that advice. This was the result of his obstinacy.

After worshipping the Lord, Dhruva felt very ashamed of the material demands he had previously decided to make. Condemning himself, he spoke thus, 'To get to see the Lord and bathe in His affectionate glances is not something ordinary. But I got such a fortune only within six months. Yet, due to my flawed mindset, I'm most unfortunate. I approached the Lord who can cut the chain of repeated birth and death and award liberation to His devotees. But out of my foolishness, I prayed for perishable things. I'm like a person who gives up diamonds for some broken pieces of glass, attracted by their glitter. Although the Lord can offer me His personal service, I wanted only material name, fame and prosperity. My case is like a poor man who goes to an emperor and asks for a few broken grains of husked rice, although the emperor can provide unlimited wealth. Material happiness is no better than pieces of glass or broken grains.'

> *One who maintains selfish ambitions ends up in dissatisfaction. But one who is selfless in one's dealings with people and the Lord experiences nourishing relationships.*

Dhruva regretted his not being able to accept good advice. 'I could not accept the genuine instructions of sage Narada. Instead, I demanded him to fulfil my ambitions with a corrupted mind. I behaved stubbornly while under an illusion. With impaired vision, I saw my brother as my enemy and my stepmother as an object of my envy. This perspective of seeing people as friends and enemies on a material plane is inappropriate.'

> *Friends and enemies in this world are created by one's own mind. Everyone is a child of God and a spiritual being; thus, we are all eternally related to each other as God's children. But because of qualities like pride, envy, greed, anger and so on, we sometimes consider others as enemies.*

In this way, Dhruva regretted his foolish mentality and the material desires he formerly maintained in his heart.

The Purifying Potency of Devotion

Those who selflessly serve Lord Vishnu or Krishna, worship Him with devotion and meditate on Him with love and affection are the most advanced devotees. However, many people approach Him to fulfil their material desires. But the specialty of the Lord is that even if one approaches Him for material motives, He gives them spiritual fulfilment, which in turn develops a sense of compunction for their material desires within them.

Although Lord Vishnu had bestowed upon Dhruva great material prosperity, Dhruva found no pleasure in it. Instead, he felt guilty for having desired such material boons. One who approaches the Lord for material pleasures will be dealt with by the Lord in such a way that they give up their taste for material enjoyment and embrace spiritual happiness.

> *Bhakti unto the Lord satisfies the heart of anyone who approaches Him with spiritual bliss so that they give up the petty, fleeting pleasures of this world.*

If we attempt to please the Lord to the best of our capacity, the power of bhakti will purify our sinful intentions. The process of bhakti is so marvellous, universal and sublime that it accommodates all kinds of worshippers, irrespective of their backgrounds. So even if we approach Krishna with impure intentions, Krishna will decontaminate them and qualify us for pure devotional service. That is the greatness of bhakti.

Worshipping Krishna is the highest beneficial activity for humanity. No matter what the objective is.

Thereafter Dhruva silently returned home. How would his father, Uttanapada, receive him? What would be the response of his beloved mother, Suniti? How would Suruchi react to Dhruva's success? How would the kingdom and the citizens welcome Dhruva? Read forward to unveil the answers.

* **

Pearls of Wisdom

Relationship Sutras

1. Selflessness enlivens relationships while selfishness estranges them.
2. Disapproval of others' misdeeds is necessary but disowning them is not.
3. Pride and envy taint our vision with negativity.
4. Time is that bandit who forcibly strips us away of everything. Accumulate that which is theft-proof.

Success Sutras

1. Determination means to terminate our temptations. Guidance means finding out how to do so.
2. When we humbly seek blessings, we purchase success at a discount.
3. The resurgence of our need for gratification in this world shows how transient it is.
4. Be desirous of satisfaction in devotion, not fleeting pleasures in oblivion.
5. Bring God to the foreground of your life, no matter what your background is.

9

Mother—Seed of Son's Success

A truly successful person is genuinely grateful to those who have guided, inspired and assisted in attaining the goal. A mother is the foremost among them.

'Your Majesty, all good fortune unto you. Your son Dhruva is returning home from the forest.' A messenger delivered this enlivening piece of information to King Uttanapada.

Uttanapada couldn't believe his ears. His son, who had strayed into the forest all by himself, was now treading homeward. The king thought the wilderness to be too much for his son to survive—the perils and wild animals posed too great a danger to his five-year-old. All this while, he was apprehensive of his son's homecoming. But now, simply the thought of seeing his son again brought the king boundless joy.

Although trusting the messenger's words seemed difficult, Uttanapada remembered what Narada Muni had spoken earlier. He had predicted Dhruva's return and success in his mission of pleasing Lord Vishnu. The king had full faith in Narada's predictions.

Delighted with the news, Uttanapada offered the messenger a valuable necklace as a token of gratitude. 'Please take this. You have made my day with this auspicious news.'

The Epitome of Tolerance and Forgiveness

Since the day Dhruva had left the palace, Uttanapada had been struck by moral scruples and had thus started favouring Dhruva's mother, Suniti. He no longer remained Suruchi's henpecked husband. After all, Suruchi's harshness and proud behaviour compelled Dhruva to leave the palace. Of course, Uttanapada's neglect was also a reason, but now he genuinely repented for his mistake. In fact, he disapproved of Suruchi's misbehaviour, something he had failed to do earlier.

The tense situation in Uttanapada's family was known to everyone. All the residents of the palace and the citizens were well aware of the reason for Dhruva's departure from the palace.

While Suruchi had always been envious, suppressive and rude, Suniti's tolerance, compassion, non-envious nature and dependence on Lord Vishnu's mercy set her apart from Suruchi. Suniti believed that no one could trouble her without the Supreme Lord's sanction. She considered all her pains to be the result of her past misdeeds. Her fortitude had thus far shielded her from the onslaughts of her husband's neglect and the discourteous behaviour of her co-wife. Therefore, Suniti went through all of this without complaining or grudging.

> *The heaviest thing to hold is a 'grudge'. One who gets rid of this heavy weight naturally feels light at heart and can relish healthy relationships.*

Noble-hearted Suniti was never spiteful to Suruchi and Uttama. Even before or after the departure of Dhruva, she never hated Suruchi. It was Suruchi who envied Suniti. The benevolent nature of Suniti and the change in Uttanapada's conduct brought a positive transformation in Suruchi. She shed off her envy towards Suniti and her tendency to control Uttanapada.

> *Noble-hearted are those who never hold any grudges, hatred, envy or negative feelings, even towards those who hate them. This eventually can bring about a transformative change in others as well. But even if it doesn't, the unenvious remain peaceful.*

Which mother can tolerate and forgive the person who separated her from her child? But broadminded Suniti had a forgiving heart that could excuse and accommodate Suruchi, who was the cause of her son's departure. Thus, she became the epitome of tolerance and forgiveness.

One who forbears difficulties and is able to forgive an offender, pleases the Lord and establishes lasting relationships.

In one sense, Suruchi's harsh words catalysed Dhruva's determination in his bhakti unto Lord Vishnu. From a positive perspective, Suruchi indirectly contributed to Dhruva's success. Therefore, there was no reason for Suniti to hate her. Even before Dhruva's departure, Suniti requested Dhruva to see the good in Suruchi's words—'If you want to sit on your father's lap, you need to worship Lord Vishnu and take shelter in my womb in your next birth!'

One with a positive outlook and the ability to see good in others attains peace and happiness even amidst the most distressful conditions.

An Exemplary Mother of a Hero

Naturally, the mother is the first teacher of a child. A child meets several other teachers only after being trained in basic culture and values by his or her own mother. We can never repay our mother's debt. A mother extends herself beyond all boundaries only to keep her child comfortable, even at the cost of bearing personal inconvenience. A mother's sacrifice to give birth and raise a child is unparalleled.

Certainly, the mother nourishes the child's physical, mental and intellectual growth. However, the specialty of Suniti is that in addition to doing everything a mother does, she also acted as her son's spiritual teacher.

The best mother supports and encourages the child to take God's shelter.

When Dhruva was overwhelmed with grief, pained and disappointed for being disallowed to sit on his father's lap, it was Suniti who inspired him to take shelter of Lord Vishnu.

Such was the greatness of Queen Suniti, the mother of a great devotee Dhruva, who became successful in pleasing the Lord within only six months. The credit for Dhruva's success certainly goes to his mother, apart from his guru, Narada Muni. In fact, even before Narada Muni taught Dhruva the process of worshipping Lord Vishnu, it was Suniti who taught him bhakti.

An Earnest Reception

Being very eager to see his long-lost son, King Uttanapada at once mounted a chariot drawn by excellent horses bedecked with golden filigree. He also took with him many brahmanas who were chanting auspicious Vedic mantras to welcome Dhruva. Several elderly members of Uttanapada's family, his officers, ministers, friends and servants also accompanied him to welcome the prince warmly. As Uttanapada proceeded in the parade, the auspicious sounds of conch shells, kettledrums and flutes made for an atmosphere of auspiciousness and good fortune.

Receiving the news of Dhruva's success and arrival, Suniti was delighted. Her happiness knew no bounds. Suniti got into a royal palanquin to receive her son. She also lovingly invited Suruchi and her son Uttama to accompany her in the palanquin. Suniti, Suruchi and Uttama got into the same palanquin and joined the procession along with Uttanapada to receive Dhruva.

Upon seeing Dhruva approaching closer, King Uttanapada got down from his chariot hastily. He had been extremely anxious to see his son for a long time. Then, with love and affection overwhelming his heart, he embraced his little boy. Struggling to breathe, he collected his son in his arms and practically bathed him with his tears.

Dhruva was no longer the passionate, ambitious, vengeful child he was six months ago. Now, he was an exalted, realized devotee of Lord Vishnu who was completely sanctified by his sincere spiritual practice. Further, he was also purified by the touch of the lotus feet of Lord Vishnu and His divine conch shell.

> *One who even remembers the Lord is purified of all sins and contamination. What then to speak of directly seeing, touching and being touched by the Lord.*

Dhruva's fortune was clearly immeasurable. With his spiritual glory, he bedazzled all the citizens of King Uttanapada. The reunion with Dhruva fulfilled Uttanapada's long-standing desire and he continuously bathed him with torrents of cold tears—tears of joy and love. Dhruva humbly and gently bowed down to his father's feet, who then put various questions about his stay in the forest before him. Dhruva answered all those questions and briefly narrated how he met Narada Muni and worshipped Lord Vishnu in the divine forest of Madhuvana on the bank of Yamuna.

The Son Coronated by Mother's Love

Dhruva bowed down at his beloved mother's feet and she blessed the child wholeheartedly with teary eyes. Suniti, the glorious mother of the little hero Dhruva, embraced her son, who was dearer to her than her own life. Seeing him, she forgot all the grief that she had been experiencing in the time gone by. Now, she was extremely pleased. When Dhruva left home, she almost fainted in separation from him. But now, she felt as if she had regained her life.

Out of intense motherly affection, milk started flowing from her breasts and soon wetted Dhruva's body. The torrents of happy tears coming from her eyes also drenched Dhruva. This was a great auspicious sign. This indicated that Dhruva would soon become the king and his *abhisheka* would be conducted. Abhisheka or the bathing ceremony, is an auspicious ritual that is carried out at the time of coronating a capable person as the ruler of an empire. Now Dhruva's mother had already performed the abhisheka and in the future, his father Uttanapada was sure to instate him as king.

Dhruva, who had become spiritually successful by pleasing the Lord, would now also be materially successful by efficiently ruling the earth. This journey of Dhruva started off with his mother's blessings. Everyone praised Suniti as the mother of a great hero. Her inspiration, guidance and devotion had made Dhruva successful.

A mother's heartfelt blessing is a great key to success.

The positive change in the characters of the henpecked king Uttanapada and haughty queen Suruchi, was mainly due to the mature outlook of Suniti, the mother of our determined hero Dhruva. She was the woman behind the success of Dhruva.

Determination vs Destiny

By and large, people gravitate to the terms 'destiny' or 'karma' to describe the way life unfolds. 'Fate' and 'luck' are synonymous with this unpacking of life. But a careful and logical analysis of this subject reveals deeper truths.

What is the true meaning of *destiny*?—In essence, destiny is the result of our past actions. Take for instance, a student who hasn't studied well through the academic year and spent his time watching random movies, browsing the internet, playing video games and so on. Then, he or she would be destined to perform poorly in his examinations. As a result, if the student tries to cheat during the exams and is found using unfair means, destiny would appear more ruthless than ever. If this insincerity is what the student carries forward in life, he would soon find his career in tatters. All this is understood to be the result of the student's actions—karma or destiny as we know it. This, to a considerable extent remains unchanging.

Destiny is a 'result' of one's past actions. That means that our current actions will be decisive in shaping our destiny that is soon to manifest. However, while experiencing the results of our past actions, one still has the independence or freewill to make choices and perform those actions that shall create one's future destiny.

For example, due to one's past unhealthy habits and irregulated actions, a man may be diagnosed with a disease. This he cannot change. But the actions that he performs after being diagnosed with the disease are in his hands. He can take proper medicines, have a healthy diet, do some exercise and pray for God's grace. Due to these careful actions, his future may be changed and he might recover. Thus, the disease that could not be reversed immediately, can be cured based on the actions that the person performs. But if he sticks to his unhealthy habits, it can worsen his health.

A businessman who has made a choice of purchasing an air ticket to Delhi and boards the Delhi flight, is *destined* to reach Delhi, not Mumbai. While travelling in the Delhi flight, he may *desire* to go to Mumbai, but he cannot ask the cabin crew to change the course of the airplane towards Mumbai. He has to reach Delhi first and can then take another flight to Mumbai. But while travelling in the Delhi flight, he has the independence to read a newspaper, listen to some music, study a book, watch a video, or make a friend with a co-passenger, make plans for his business expansion, and so on, and create his further destiny.

So, all of us have some 'destiny' to experience, and some 'freewill' or 'independence' to make choices and perform actions to create one's further destiny. Our current conscious choices and determined actions can be in the direction of creating a bright future for ourselves and near and dear ones.

One may experience one's destiny, but by following a spiritual path and worshiping the Lord with determination, one gets the inner strength to not get overwhelmed by the ill effects of one's destiny and further be successful in creating a great future of attaining the Lord. That's the real success of human life.

Who Is Entitled to Credit for Your Success?

Our success is not always a result of our own determined endeavours. The credit for our success also goes to the desires, efforts and blessings of several well-wishers, parents, teachers and everyone who helped us in various ways. So, one should not be greedy to snatch away all the credit one's success brings.

> *The real success is to remain humble and grounded when successful and be grateful to those who helped us to be successful.*
>
> *One who does not acknowledge the help and support offered by others in attaining success is an*

ungrateful person. Mother Earth cannot tolerate the burden of an ungrateful person.

There have been many heroes in this world but there is no comparison to Dhruva. He was not only a heroic emperor but also a great devotee. He had conquered his senses and mind and attained the unfathomable goal of pleasing Lord Vishnu within six months. He was the worthy son of a devoted mother and the exemplary disciple of a great guru. He brought glory to the name, fame and prestige of his parents and teachers.

We too must act, speak and think in a way that increases the honour of our elders. Our thoughts, words and actions should not bring them infamy. Dhruva, although very young, made all of his elders and even the citizens of his kingdom proud.

One person's success can make many people happy.

Everyone was pleased with Dhruva. But what was Suruchi's reaction? How did Dhruva treat Suruchi? How did she perceive his success? What was the reaction of Uttama, Dhruva's stepbrother? Flip the page to find out.

* * *

Pearls of Wisdom

Relationship Sutras

1. Be grateful to those who guided, inspired and supported you. Start with your mother.
2. Get rid of the heavy weight of 'grudges' to lighten your heart.
3. Deal with the hateful without hatred.
4. Forgiveness is a charity that very few can afford.
5. Try to forgive, to be forgiven.
6. Seek transformation of the poor-hearted, not their destruction.
7. Cultivate forbearance amidst inevitable reversals.
8. When you see good in others, you replicate how God sees you.

Success

1. A mother's heartfelt blessing is a great key to success.
2. Your success makes many happy.
3. Life is like a trampoline—the more you push down your ego, the higher you'll fly.
4. Let your success make others happy but don't equate making others happy with success.
5. A mother can play the role of a mentor, father, brother and whatnot. Can anyone repay her?

10

Good Attracts Good Will

One who really loves God loves those who love God and those whom God loves. Thus, a lover of God has the best loving relationships in this world.

Dhruva respectfully bowed to his stepmother Suruchi, who had inflicted great pain upon him earlier. When a person sees his tormentor, such a vision can be intolerable, what to speak of exchanging pleasantries?

But Dhruva had absolutely no hesitation in touching the feet of Suruchi. This was because he no longer maintained any grudge, hatred or envy toward her. In fact, Dhruva had absolutely no bitter feelings towards anyone in the world. This change in him resulted from his mature devotion to Lord Vishnu. This is the nature of a devotee.

One who loves God cannot hate anyone. After all, a lover of God understands and acknowledges that everyone is a child of God.

Envy Transformed into Affection

Suruchi was touched to see the innocent boy falling at her feet. With great motherly affection, she immediately picked him up. She embraced him with tears of love and blessed him, saying, 'My dear boy, may you live long.'

The same Suruchi had earlier told Dhruva that his life was worthless because he did not have the opportunity and fortune of even sitting on his father's lap or throne. She indirectly suggested that he die and be reborn in her womb to qualify to sit on his father's lap. Now, the same woman blessed him to live long. This power of bhakti revolutionized the hearts of both Dhruva and Suruchi, who, at one point in time, envied each other bitterly.

True Love in Relationships

It was the devotion to the Lord within the heart of Suniti that reverberated in the hearts of Dhruva, Uttanapada and Suruchi.

Just as water flows naturally from top to bottom, all living beings naturally love a person with whom the Lord is pleased.

A devotee develops friendliness towards all living beings. A loving bonding between a devotee and other living beings organically blossoms.

Therefore, when our relationships with others are based on our love for the Lord, we identify others as God's beloved children. Such a relationship is a spiritual one that immensely nourishes the heart and soul.

Dhruva then saw his stepbrother, Uttama, the son of Suruchi, and soon tears began blurring his vision. Even Uttama had tears of affection in his eyes as he saw his elder brother. Six months ago, Dhruva had been jealous of Uttama but now, being purified of all jealousy and anger, Dhruva embraced Uttama out of great brotherly affection.

The residents of Uttanapada's palace praised queen Suniti, 'Dear queen, your beloved son had departed a long time ago and it is your good fortune that he has now come back. Your son will surely be able to protect you for a long time and will put an end to all your miseries. Moreover, he will protect the whole earth. You must have worshipped Lord Vishnu with deep devotion and dedication for those who constantly meditate upon Him, surpass all dangers. You have turned your son into a great devotee, which is extraordinary.'

While everyone was thus praising Dhruva and Suniti, King Uttanapada became joyous. He seated Dhruva and Uttama on the back of a cow elephant. Thus, he returned to his capital along with his two queens, who were now great friends.

The Key to a Happy Family Life

The family of Uttanapada, which was once filled with anxieties, tensions and bitter feelings, had now been converted into a happy family. Earlier, the members of this family—a husband, two wives, and two children—suffered from strained relationships. There was an absence of a loving bond. Their relationships lacked nourishment. One party's envy, pride and arrogance resulted in tears, lamentation and pain in the other. While irresponsibility and weakness of the heart overruled Uttanapada, the family that lived in an opulent palace amidst hundreds of servants only dreamt of happiness and cordial relations.

But now, the same family had been transformed into a loving family composed of sweet and wholesome relationships. The hearts of all five members of the family had now been strung together.

Suruchi had acted impulsively owing to her pride and envy. Uttanapada behaved imprudently due to his attachment to his wife. Dhruva's material ambitions had made him obstinate. In essence, it was Suniti only who acted maturely due to her devotion to Lord Vishnu.

Because Suniti herself was a devotee, she could inspire Dhruva to take to bhakti. Although Dhruva was ambitious, the guidance he received from great devotees like Suniti and Narada purified and elevated him. Although Uttanapada neglected his chaste wife and noble son, he honestly repented for his mistakes and soon embraced conduct. Although Suruchi was envious and proud, the kindness of Suniti and the spiritual success of Dhruva 'positivized' her as well. It was Suniti's tolerance and devotion that ultimately brought transformation across her entire family. By analysing the characters of all these personalities in this story, we can understand the glory of bhakti.

Bhakti, or devotion unto the Lord, ultimately brings about ideal transformation in oneself and others.

Even one person in a family who is in positive spirits can make the entire family happy and satisfied.

When God takes centre stage in one's home, distresses get scared to even knock on the door.

Unparalleled Royal Opulence

On receiving Dhruva at the city's outskirts, Uttanapada's family happily entered the gigantic flamboyant city that was decorated with columns of banana trees laden with fruits and flowers. At each gate were present, auspiciously burning lamps and big water pots decorated with colourful clothes, strings of pearls, flower garlands and mango leaves. In the city were several palaces, city gates and surrounding walls which were tremendously beautiful.

On the occasion of Dhruva's welcome, the domes of the city palaces glittered and beautiful airborne chariots hovered above the city. All the lanes and streets of the city, and the raised sitting places at road crossings were thoroughly cleansed and sprinkled with sandalwood water. Grains like rice and barley, flowers and fruits and other auspicious articles were scattered throughout the city.

Dhruva passed on the road from every place in the neighbourhood. Some gentle household ladies assembled to see him. Out of motherly affection, they offered him their blessings and showered him with auspicious articles like mustard seed, barley, yogurt, water, newly grown grasses, flowers and fruits. In this way, little Dhruva, while hearing the pleasing song sung by these ladies, entered the palace of his father, Uttanapada.

Uttanapada's palace walls were ornamented with priceless gems. The bedding in the palace was as white as the foam of milk and exceedingly soft. The bedsteads were cast in ivory with embellishments of gold. The chairs, benches and other seating were furnished in gold. The palace was surrounded by walls made of marble with many engravings decorated with valuable jewels like sapphires. These inscriptions depicted beautiful women with shining gemstone lamps in their hands.

The palace was surrounded by gardens, filled with varieties of trees obtained from different heavenly planets. In those trees were pairs of sweetly singing birds and mad bumblebees, which made harmonious buzzing sounds. There were emerald staircases which led to lakes full of colourful lotuses and lilies. Swans and other beautiful birds playfully sported in those lakes.

Growing up in this ambience, Dhruva bathed in the love of his father, mother and brother. The success he attained nourished him spiritually, enlivened his family life and made it more fulfilling.

Absorption and devotion bring one spiritual satisfaction and the bliss of loving friendships and relationships.

Balancing Responsibility and Detachment

When Dhruva grew up and became sufficiently mature as a young man, King Uttanapada considered enthroning him as the king. He consulted his ministers to determine if Dhruva could take charge of the kingdom. All his ministers, well-wishers and guides unanimously agreed to coronate Dhruva. The citizens of the kingdom were also glad to have Dhruva as their emperor.

Thus, Uttanapada decided to crown Dhruva and retire from his kingly responsibilities. Uttanapada wished to dedicate his life to the welfare of his spiritual self. He wanted to detach himself from his family, political and other worldly affairs. He thus decided to leave the palace and enter the forest. In the forest, he desired to worship Lord Vishnu and attain Vaikuntha—his life's goal.

On that providential day, Uttanapada enthroned Dhruva, proclaiming the beginning of his reign. At that time, Dhruva was unmarried. But Uttanapada did not wait for Dhruva to be married. He understood that Dhruva was mature and capable of taking care of himself. He knew Dhruva would do the needful in his personal life and protect his citizens. Uttanapada showered Dhruva with his blessings and retired from the kingdom, unable to delay his spiritual life anymore.

Uttanapada was a *rajarshi*. Raja means king and rishi means saint. Rajarshi refers to a saintly king. Rajarshis, despite possessing the capabilities of a king, are also saintly in their character. Scriptures like the Srimad Bhagavatam narrate stories of saintly kings who ruled the earth righteously while caring for their citizens' material and spiritual needs. Whenever an able successor was ready to take charge of the royal responsibilities, these kings, despite their great influence, followers, accomplishments and unexcelled comforts were detached and mature enough to leave behind everything for a higher purpose. They would promptly retire at the right time to dedicate the rest of their lives in devotion unto the Lord or one of His forms—Vishnu, Krishna, Rama, Narasimha and so on.

Responsibility shouldn't lead to undue attachment and detachment doesn't equate to irresponsibility.

Thus, Rajarshis, or saintly kings, teach us the right balance between responsibility and detachment by example. For instance, King Yudhisthira ruled the kingdom responsibly in line with the knowledge he had received from Lord Krishna. Yudhisthira raised his grandson Parikshit with suitable training and entrusted the kingdom to him just before he retired. Several other saintly kings, like Priyavrata, Uttanapada, Dhruva, Prithu, Bharata and Parikshit, have also exemplified detachment. These kings gloriously departed this world and later entered the spiritual world. Unsurprisingly, Dhruva would take forward the same legacy.

Saintly kings rule with responsibility and retire with detachment as soon as an able successor is ready to take charge of the citizens and kingdom. They don't greedily hold on to their posts till the fag end of life.

Learned souls master the art of empowering successors at the appropriate time without insecurity.

The success of human life is not in holding on to things till the far end of life but in relinquishing things at the appropriate time to pursue higher goals.

Thus, we come to the end of Dhruva's early life and the section entitled 'A Determined Prince'.

But how did King Dhruva maintain his kingdom? How did he deal with his citizens and family?

Before other questions trouble your mind, let's quench the thirst of your curiosity by switching sections and seeing how life progressed for Dhruva as a king. And by the time you get to the last leaf, you'll have answers to questions—big, small or even unasked and that's a promise!

* * *

Pearls of Wisdom

Relationship Sutras

1. When the vision of seeing everyone as God's child anoints your eyes, developing soulful relations doesn't take much effort.
2. Become a lover of God to love everyone and be loved by everyone.
3. Devotion doesn't stop the rains of distress but it equips you with an umbrella.
4. Positive spirits pave the way for satisfying relations.

Success Sutras

1. Absorption and devotion in a positive action bring satisfaction.
2. Make sure your 'responsibility' doesn't become an 'attachment.'
3. Make sure your 'detachment' doesn't become 'irresponsibility.'
4. Empower successors at an appropriate time.
5. Don't be too possessive about temporary possessions or positions.
6. Relinquish positions and possessions at the right time to pursue higher goals.

SECTION II

AN EFFICIENT EMPEROR

11

The Pain of Losing a Companion

Philosophical understanding is not meant to eliminate our emotions but to channelize them, so that we don't become dysfunctional, by being emotional.

After the departure of Uttanapada, King Dhruva married Bhrami, the daughter of Prajapati Shisumara. Dhruva and Bhrami had two sons named Kalpa and Vatsara. The greatly powerful Dhruva had another wife named Ila, the daughter of Vayudev, the wind god. Dhruva and Ila had a son named Utkala and a beautiful daughter. Thus, Dhruva lived happily in his kingdom along with his two wives, three sons and a daughter.

Two Back-to-Back Deaths!

One day, Dhruva's younger brother Uttama, who was still unmarried, set out on a hunting excursion. While hunting in the forest, a powerful Yaksha from the Himalayan Mountains killed Uttama. When this news reached Suruchi, she became perturbed and disoriented. She immediately headed to the forest searching for her son and was soon consumed by a forest fire. This is how Suruchi met her death. These events were foretold by Lord Vishnu when he had appeared before Dhruva after his six-month-long tapasya.

But how could Suruchi and Uttama meet such a ghastly death? How could they be punished so severely for their offence towards Dhruva, which they had rectified later? Although Suruchi insulted Dhruva once, she was later transformed and became affectionate towards Dhruva like a mother. It is quite evident that Suruchi's heart was transformed by the good nature of Suniti and the spiritual success attained by Dhruva. Uttama had neither verbally nor physically offended Dhruva. Does this mean one would have to undergo the reaction to one's past misdeeds even after repenting and rectifying them? How could the Lord ordain such a death upon these transformed personalities?

The grisly death of Suruchi and Uttama seemed to be a reaction to their sins committed in the past, but due to their relationship with Dhruva, their souls were undoubtedly elevated. On the worldly plane, to the eyes of the people, they were experiencing reactions to their mistakes. This is because the Lord may have wanted to teach a lesson to all of us through them, i.e., offending a devotee or anyone unnecessarily would lead to undesirable effects. However, at the same time, the Lord would have been supremely merciful upon them due to the transformation they had undergone.

After Dhruva's success in pleasing Lord Vishnu, Dhruva treated Suruchi and Uttama with warmth and care, who in turn, treated Dhruva similarly. They shared a loving relationship with a great devotee like Dhruva. Certainly, the Lord would not plunge the souls of Suruchi and Uttama into hell but would have given them a better destination in their next life.

What is visible to our material eyes is not always the truth.

Apparently, the Lord might put good people or even pure devotees in some awkward situation, but that is only to teach a lesson to the common people. This does not mean that the Lord is not kind.

The Anguish of a Loving Heart

When the news of Uttama's death at the hands of a Yaksha reached the ears of Dhruva, his mind was deluged with lamentation and anger. Immediately picking up his bow and arrows, he got onto his chariot to fight with the Yakshas. He rushed towards the Alakapuri region in the Himalayas—the abode of the Yakshas.

How could Dhruva get infuriated so easily? He was a pure devotee who had had darshan of Lord Vishnu and was destined to go to Vaikuntha at the age of five. Was it appropriate on his part to become enraged and emotional upon the death of his brother?

One of the great teachings of the scriptures is to tolerate happiness and distress, success and failure, victory and defeat, and other such dualities in life because of their temporary nature. They come and go and have no permanent effect. From that perspective, Dhruva's lamentation of the death of Uttama seems surprising. But at the same time, it also appears to be unsurprising. How so?!

Spiritualists understand the philosophy and try to be neutral and equipoised amidst various difficulties in life. However, they are not stone-hearted emotionless entities. They, too, have appropriate emotions. Although devotees understand the philosophy that the soul is eternal and the body is temporary, still, at some point in life, devotees become distressed when they lose their beloved ones.

> *A spiritualist's lamentation on the death of a friend is not a lack of understanding of the science of the soul but organic love for the departed soul.*

They miss the association of their beloved ones from whose company they received unlimited inspiration. Therefore, it is natural even for devotees to lament.

> *Philosophical understanding should not make one stone-hearted but should make one soft-hearted.*

Dhruva was pining for his beloved brother Uttama, and wanted to avenge his death. Further, as a king, it was his responsibility to punish an offender who had unceremoniously killed his brother. So, at this moment, Dhruva's anger was appropriate and justified.

He then journeyed to the north, to the city of Yakshas. The Yakshas were ghostly followers of Lord Shiva who stayed in the Alakapuri region, in the Himalayan Valley. They were endowed with several mystical powers.

But didn't Dhruva already know that Uttama would die in this way? The Lord had personally predicted before him. Then, how could Dhruva react with such intensity upon hearing about his brother's death? He was outraged—his grief and anger drove him to ferocity. This was because Dhruva had only affection for Uttama now, although Dhruva was jealous of him in the past. Perhaps Dhruva would have seemed vengeful towards Uttama had he not avenged Uttama's death this way. Therefore, Dhruva's anger was justified.

What happened at Alakapuri, the capital of the Yakshas? Would Dhruva be successful in punishing the Yakshas? Or would he be defeated by their prowess? Hold tight and read forward as you uncover the battle of Dhruva and the Yakshas.

* * *

Pearls of Wisdom

Relationship Sutras

1. Never give up your love for your dear ones and tag it as philosophy.
2. Spirituality arrests attachment and embraces emotion.

12

Battle with the Inner Enemies

Overcoming a few obstacles and tasting a little success can boost our confidence, but that shouldn't make us boastful and negligent, for the journey still remains.

Upon reaching Alakapuri, Dhruva sounded his conch shell. The sound of his conch shell resonated throughout the region, petrifying the Yakshas and their wives. The sound travelled across miles and completely smashed the peace of Alakapuri to smithereens.

The Yakshas understood this war cry. The powerful Yaksha heroes could not tolerate such a courageous invasion of their city. Although they became greatly frightened just by hearing the sound of Dhruva's conch shell, they still came out of their city with weapons to attack Dhruva.

Dhruva was a great charioteer and certainly a great bowman as well. He immediately picked up his arrows to attack the Yakshas. He released three arrows at a time and pierced the bodies of hundreds of Yakshas effortlessly. This expertise in Dhruva's martial skills impressed the Yakshas heroes and they even praised him. It is natural for a kshatriya hero to honestly praise the prowess of even their enemy.

An Attack That Increased the Enthusiasm

The Yakshas, 1,30,000 in number, very strong and invincible, then counter-attacked Dhruva. Just like serpents, who cannot tolerate being trampled by the feet of someone, they couldn't tolerate Dhruva's attack and began shooting twice as many arrows as Dhruva. Each Yaksha began releasing six arrows at a time, while Dhruva responded with three shots.

Dhruva was fighting them alone while the Yakshas, a formidably large group of enemies, incessantly showered upon Dhruva and his chariot their razor-sharp arrows. Dhruva was thus completely covered by arrows, just like a mountain overspread with unabating rainfall. However, just as a mountain is unaffected by the torrents of rain that fall upon it, Dhruva was undeterred by the shower of arrows. In fact, Dhruva's determination and competency increased by such an efficient counter-attack from his enemies. His enthusiasm for fighting got rejuvenated. This is indeed a success formula.

The inevitable obstacles in our attempts shouldn't demotivate us, rather, they must revivify our enthusiasm to overcome them and attain success in our endeavour.

When the clouds shower torrents of rain on a mountain, not only does the mountain remain unaffected but it also becomes cleansed of all dirt. Nobody would ever wash off the dirt on the surface of the mountain. But rains do, leaving the mountain clean and shiny. The trees and plants on the mountain become nourished and the mountain appears lush green. Similarly, Dhruva was compared to a mountain because his enthusiasm to fight was magnified as a result of his enemies' attack.

Upon observing Dhruva being covered by an unending line of arrows, the residents of the upper planets roared in astonishment and anxiety. 'Alas, the grandson of Svayambhuva Manu, Dhruva, is now lost.' As they cried in this way, Dhruva, just like the rising sun, rose above the ocean of the Yakshas. This display of courage and valour left the celestial beings speechless.

Unparalleled Heroism

The Yakshas, having gained the upper hand, exclaimed, for they believed they had conquered Dhruva. But, in the meantime, Dhruva's chariot, just like the sun that suddenly appeared from within the foggy mist, materialized before the Yakshas. The mist seems to cover the sun, but, in truth, fog is insignificant compared to the sun. Only our eyes are affected by the presence of fog or clouds but the sun is uninfluenced.

Thus, Dhruva just as the shining sun easily cleared away the fog of the Yaksha's weapons. The twanging and hissing of Dhruva's bow and arrows terrorized the hearts of the Yakshas. He began shooting arrows unstoppably and soon Dhruva shattered all of the Yakshas' weaponry just like the wind that scatters the clouds in the sky.

Dhruva's sharp arrows cruised through the shields and bodies of the Yakshas. Heads were severed and fell to the ground. The bodies of the Yakshas were actually decorated with shining earrings, turbans, bracelets and armlets. On their heads were very valuable crowns. All these ornaments now lay scattered on the battlefield. This sight pleased the kshatriya hero, Dhruva.

Silence on the battlefield

The Yakshas who survived Dhruva's onslaught became fearful and started fleeing from the battleground. It was as if elephants were fleeing upon being defeated by a lion. Dhruva, the best of the warriors, observed that the great battlefield was devoid of any opponents and found only himself standing on the ground decorated with fallen weapons and bodily limbs of soldiers now gone. Was the fight over? What would Dhruva do now?

Dhruva then desired to enter the city of Alakapuri and explore the city. He had never visited this place before. Suddenly a thought appeared in Dhruva's mind: 'No one knows the plans of the mystic Yakshas. They fled, being unable to fight with me. They are not visible on the battlefield now. But does this mean they will resume their attack? These are mystic enemies and cannot be trusted.' In this way, Dhruva expressed his doubts about the unpredictable warfare of the Yakshas to his chariot driver.

> *One of the secrets to attaining success in one's goals is to be alert and not overconfident.*

Defeating the Yaksha soldiers was no trouble for Dhruva. Although it was so, Dhruva wasn't proud nor overconfident of his abilities. Rather, he was vigilant and careful. When the Yakshas ran away from the battlefield, Dhruva did not immediately accept his victory. Instead, he paused and reflected on the possible future course of action of the Yakshas.

> *Having crossed a few milestones in one's journey may be encouraging, but it shouldn't make one incautious for the rest of the journey.*

The greatest diversions in life are caused by the mind and the senses. All of us keep battling with our inner enemies, namely the senses and the mind. The mind is a storehouse of unlimited positive and negative impressions that keep popping and distracting us from our goals. The mind's vehemence is fulfilled through the senses, which are subservient to it. One who becomes a victim of the distracted mind and senses has no scope of success in spiritual or material life.

One might not be disturbed by one's mind and senses for some time, and in many cases, that could be a great achievement. Yet, if one becomes inattentive, the same mind and senses might make an even stronger comeback. So, it is essential to never get overconfident in one's endeavours. One must be alert and attentive like Dhruva.

Just as a warrior on the battlefield expects an attack from the enemy at any moment and thus remains alert, similarly, we need to be alert in our endeavours, knowing well that the inner enemies of complacency are more dangerous than the outer enemies.

Life is more about winning a war with internal enemies rather than struggling to defeat external enemies.

What would happen next? Would the Yakshas counter-attack Dhruva as he expected? Or would they simply accept defeat? Had the fight ended? If not, what would be its nature? Turn the page to find out.

* * *

Pearls of Wisdom

Success Sutras

1. Failures can elevate or demotivate. Craft your life as per your choice.
2. Confidence unlocks success. Overconfidence locks it.
3. Don't become incautious due to intermediate success.
4. Win over the inner enemies of complacency and inattention.
5. If failures are inevitable, success is surely perishable. Be merry, not haughty!
6. When the world seems to be full of pains, recognize them to be your mind's endless complaints. Win the war within to defeat the wars without.

13

When Wrath Crosses All Limits

Even 'anger' has its utility in relationships. One may exhibit 'controlled anger' to bring a positive change in a person or a situation, but when one becomes 'controlled by anger,' one ends up disrupting relationships.

Doubting his mystic enemies, Dhruva held his ground. As Dhruva continued expressing his doubts about his mystic enemies to his charioteer, he heard an ear-splitting sound. The sound somewhat represented the howling of a raging ocean. Carrying with it clouds of dust, a great dust storm appeared. Blanketing the sky, it began spreading out in all directions.

Within moments, dense clouds overcast the sky while tumultuous thundering rumbled through the clouds. Flashes of lightning followed a violent downpour of rain. But it wasn't water that was pouring. Raining down torrents of blood, mucus, pus, stool, urine and marrow, the sky no longer simply showered water. Human torsos began falling to the ground from the skies above. This scene perplexed Dhruva.

The Hero Becomes Scared

Wonderstruck at the occurrence of such an unnatural and unseen phenomenon, Dhruva tried making sense of the whole situation. Then, he noticed a mammoth-like mystic mountain in the sky. Startlingly, maces, swords, spiked iron clubs, lances and boulders began charging in from every direction. Flabbergasted, Dhruva lost all reason. He did not know what to do. Were these phenomena the result of the occult of the Yakshas? If yes, how would these dangers be counteracted? It is easy to battle with an enemy who stands before you but, for Dhruva, things were different. His enemy remained invisible while all he could see were their weaponry.

But this wasn't the end of the mystic display. Adding to this conundrum, huge angry-eyed serpents vomiting fire appeared at the scene. Mad elephants, lions and tigers alongside the serpents stormed towards Dhruva to devour him. The world seemed to have reached the brink of destruction. If that were not enough, a fierce ocean foaming with violent waves roared as it approached Dhruva to drown the very last of him.

Dhruva certainly expected the Yakshas to return to the battlefield. Now, his doubts about their counter-attack were materializing and the situation appeared dreadful.

> *Sometimes people follow moral codes when everything is going right. But in times of difficulty, they resort to illegal means.*

The demoniac Yakshas are, by nature, very heinous. With their illusory powers, they can create strange phenomena like these to frighten their opponent. Thus, making no attempt to counter the Yakshas' evil ambush, Dhruva looked on in bafflement. Thus, the illusive trickery of the Yakshas completely overpowered Dhruva.

Hope amidst Chaos

The great sages heard of Dhruva's predicament on the battlefield. Instantly appearing before Dhruva, they began encouraging and guiding him. Being illustrious devotees of Lord Vishnu, the sages were kind and affectionate to Dhruva, who himself was another devotee.

> *It is the nature of noble souls to voluntarily help others in difficulties, even unasked.*

Facing difficulties is natural and so is finding some support in situations like these. It is by the Lord's arrangement that one gets the necessary support from the right sources while facing adversities in life. That is the real hope amidst the chaos.

Out of great compassion, the sages began speaking to Dhruva. 'Dear Dhruva,' they said, 'O great son of King Uttanapada, may Lord Vishnu, who holds the *Saranga* bow, help you through this circumstance. The Lord is extremely merciful and only He possesses the ability to kill all your threatening enemies. His holy name is as powerful as Himself. Simply by chanting and hearing the Lord's name, countless people were easily protected from fear and death. Therefore, you must take shelter of Lord Narayana (Vishnu). With a prayerful mood, you should invoke His presence in your weapons by chanting the 'Narayana' mantra. Thus, you will be able to easily dispel all the delusions created by the demoniac Yakshas.'

The sages instructed Dhruva to chant the Lord's holy names, for only that could dispel all the spells of the Yakshas. We, too, in our spiritual life are bewildered by numerous allurements that come our way. In such situations, it is our like-minded association that comes forward to our assistance.

Devotee association offers us one of the greatest supports by inspiring us to take shelter of the Lord's holy name.

Power of Well-Wishers

Dhruva felt grateful for the voluntary assistance he received from the great sages. This was a burst of encouragement he had gotten in an hour of crisis. Sometimes, we may have all the knowledge and intelligence to solve our problems, but the right kind of ideas may not come to our minds in the right time.

Sometimes the problems we face can be so overwhelming that we may not be able to apply the solutions despite knowing them. It is at such times that the need for a well-wishing friend is felt the most.

Our good attitude and behaviour are the keys to cultivating lifelong relationships and enlivening friendships that support us through testing times.

Success is not simply the result of knowledge but also the heartfelt wishes and support of our well-wishers. One who values relationships can easily find good-hearted people who make life truly fulfilling.

Therefore, success cannot be purchased with one's individual endeavours. We are dependent on multiple hands and heads to attain success. The right kind of association, guidance and support from well-wishers paves the way to success. Thus, a vital aspect of success in life is to have cordial relationships with well-wishers and friends, who are unenvious and have the heart to celebrate our success.

The selfless sages assembled on the battlefield to assist Dhruva were such kind of people. In fact, they were kind and affectionate towards him.

The support that is given without being requested for is real and selfless.

When the Human Is Supported by the Divine

Dhruva then took up his arrow and fixed it on his bow. That arrow was no ordinary one. It was the powerful

Narayanastra, the weapon made by Lord Narayana. As soon as Dhruva fixed the Narayanastra on his bow, all the illusions created by the Yakshas were immediately vanquished! Several arrows with golden shafts and feathers like the wings of a swan flew out from it. They penetrated through the defence of the enemy with a great hissing sound, just like the tumultuous crowing of peacocks that sometimes frightens the fine-hearted. Similarly, the arrows released by Dhruva horrified the hearts of all the Yaksha soldiers.

As the sharp arrows dismayed the enemy soldiers leaving them unconscious, a handful of survivors somehow collected their weapons and came back at Dhruva. Just as serpents agitated by the mighty eagle Garuda rush towards the mighty eagle with upraised hoods, all the Yaksha soldiers prepared to overcome Dhruva with their upraised weapons.

Seeing the Yakshas rushing towards him, Dhruva immediately took up his arrows and cut his enemies to pieces. He severed their arms, legs, heads and bellies from their bodies within no time. He could not keep a count of how many Yakshas he was killing. In this way, Dhruva seemed to have crossed all limits!

Anger, when unchecked, keeps on increasing.

Can One Person's Mistake Make Many Culprits?

But why, in the first place, did Dhruva lock horns with the Yakshas? It was only one of those Yakshas who killed his brother Uttama, not all of them. Considering this, is it reasonable that Dhruva kills hundreds and thousands of the Yaksha clan for the mistake of one among them?

It is natural to be angry with the person who hurts us. If the pain caused by someone's actions is too severe, one might even consider punishing them. But how appropriate is it to condemn or punish an entire community or a race or for one person's mistake?

Dhruva's anger was now unbridled. Having driven away the illusions of the Yakshas with the Narayanastra, Dhruva became increasingly enraged. He lost his self-control. Making a robust comeback, Dhruva began indiscriminately killing all the Yakshas until the whole Yaksha clan was nearly exterminated.

When anger takes charge, even great souls lose self-control and become subservient to their own anger.

Dhruva's fury shot to the sky. As a result of his prolonged infuriation, Dhruva lost discrimination. Dhruva, who wasn't affected by inattention earlier, was now affected by undue anger. Being a victim of excessive wrath, he started indiscriminately killing all the Yakshas, almost to the point of destroying their race entirely—all for the mistake of one Yaksha. Is it justified to kill or condemn an entire race for one person's mistake?

Earlier, when he was deluded by the illusory tricks of Yakshas, the sages saved him by reminding him of the Narayanastra. But now, when Dhruva had been victimized by his unfathomable anger, would someone be able to convince him to give it up? Would stopping Dhruva be reduced to a fantasy? Would the race of the Yakshas cease to exist? That only the next chapter can reveal.

* * *

Pearls of Wisdom

Relationship Sutras

1. Knowledge is not a replacement for the support of well-wishers.
2. Well-wishers may not praise you but they'll surely upraise you.
3. Help friends not just when they 'call' you but when they 'need' you.
4. Be selfless and expect no benefits in return.
5. Support given selflessly satisfies the heart.
6. Rejecting the entire basket of fruits just because one is rotten will make you miss the real sweetness.
7. The level of fear indicates the level of disconnect from the Supremely powerful.

Success Sutras

1. Want to dismiss peace? Then give anger a seat.
2. Check your anger before it checks you.
3. An ocean of difficulties turns into a puddle when you grab God's outstretched hands.

14

The Fortune of Timely Guidance

Where there are cordial relationships and a culture of respect, feedback and corrections are given and received with ease.

'My dear grandson, please stop. This intemperate anger does not befit you. In fact, excessive wrath opens the doors to hell. You are now overstepping all boundaries by killing even those Yakshas who have committed no offence.' Intervening in this way, Svayambhuva Manu, Dhruva's grandfather, began speaking to him.

Svayambhuva Manu was one of the first created beings in the universe. He was the direct son of Lord Brahma and the father of mankind. In fact, human beings are called *manushyas* because they're the descendants of Manu.

Seeing Dhruva's burning rage, Svayambhuva Manu had appeared with some sages to intercept the uncontrollable fury of Dhruva. Dhruva, if unchecked, would annihilate the race of the Yakshas.

Wisdom of Experienced Elders—Our Asset

Generally, it is nearly impossible for an impassioned kshatriya warrior to stop warring midway. Kshatriyas generally rebuff peace-making talks for the kshatriya way of settling disputes is engaging in battle. What then to speak of some mid-battle disarmament counsel? But as astounding as it may sound, Dhruva immediately stopped fighting and respectfully looked at Manu to hear what he had to say. He was sure that Manu wouldn't have approached him in the midst of the battle without an important reason.

> *Even the mere presence of great souls can restrain someone from doing things inappropriately.*
>
> *A culture of respecting the well-wishing elders and welcoming their wise words makes human society attractive.*

Elders have seen life a lot more than the youngsters. One of the greatest assets of the younger generation is the 'experience' of their parents, grandparents, teachers and other elders. Experienced elders are natural well-wishers of their younger ones and can guide them on the right path. Their intention is to 'Let my little one not repeat the same mistakes my colleagues and I had committed! Let me guide them while duly respecting their autonomy.'

Those who lack respect for their elders miss the opportunity of taking benefit of their wisdom and maturity.

Unfortunate are those who make mistakes due to a lack of mature guidance from experienced elders. More unfortunate are those who do not take the benefit of the wisdom of their well-wishing elders, even when it is available.

Dhruva respectfully heard his grandfather speak. Manu, too, unhesitatingly, instructed Dhruva in the middle of the battle, for he knew of his grandson's respectful, mature and dignified behaviour.

Fortunate is that person whose senior unfalteringly provides him or her constructive feedback.

Stubborn and highly opinionated people miss the golden opportunity to improve themselves despite having mature and experienced elders.

Necessity of Guidance/Culture of Respect in Relationships

Everyone in this world ought to be guided by someone. Nobody in this world can live oblivious to others. However exalted, successful and accomplished one may be, there is still a possibility of committing mistakes. Therefore, one needs seasoned advice from well-wishers to prevent errors and the need for their rectification.

Those who are humble and open to corrections from well-wishers can rectify their mistakes effectively.

For instance, even Arjuna, the most celebrated warrior of his time, was confused before the battle of Kurukshetra. Although he had received several military accolades from great devatas like Indra and Shiva, at that moment of crisis, he was stupefied. Then, his dear friend, the Almighty God Krishna, guided him, and cleared his confusion. Thus, Arjuna could discharge his duty of fighting in the war at Kurukshetra.

In this narrative, Dhruva became excessively angry and lost his discrimination in killing the Yakshas. Condemning an entire race or a community of people for one person's mistake is not approved by Manu or by any other learned authority. Therefore, Manu came to guide Dhruva.

Feedbacks in Mature Societies

Manu instructed Dhruva thus, 'Dear Dhruva, the killing of numerous Yakshas which you have undertaken is disagreeable to those in the learned circles. Indeed, our family is to be known as an upholder of *dharma*. Therefore, it is not befitting of you to commit such atrocities.'

Violence may be utilized to punish a wrongdoer. However, without good intelligence and sagaciousness, coercion could be used to create unnecessary turmoil in society. Killing may not always be unethical, yet when killing is practiced unnecessarily to harm an innocent person, such violence induces one to walk the path to hell. Only for the maintenance of law and order of the state is a kshatriya permitted to make use of such brutality. Taking to savagery capriciously is strictly forbidden.

> *Violence can be a useful instrument in the service of humanity but one needs the right discrimination and training to use it.*

Manu was confident that his words alone would be sufficient to drive back Dhruva's sword back into its sheath. In a mature human society, a well-intended word can control the sword, but, in an uncultured society, a sword becomes essential to counteract another sword.

> *The greatest crisis in human society is when its members give up their inclination to hear the mature and well-intended advice of experienced elders.*

While in a degraded society, a person has to be disciplined using coercive measures, in a mature and dignified human society, people are more refined in their dealings, behaviour and character. In such a decorous society, violence becomes needless. For instance, a notorious criminal accustomed to robbing, looting and killing people is controlled by the police by physical punishment. But a mature student may lovingly be corrected by the teachers when he makes a mistake.

While in mature circles, corrections and feedbacks are given and taken in a dignified way, in uncultured societies, feedback and corrections are given and taken in forceful ways.

Dhruva was mature. Although he had made an overwhelming number of Yakshas bite the dust, that was only a momentary emotional outburst spawned by the death of his brother. Such behaviour was not an innate aspect of his core personality.

The circumstantial outburst of great souls, who are otherwise sober, doesn't minimize their glory.

Both cultured and uncultured people make mistakes. But what differentiates one from the other is that egoistic uncultured people do not accept, admit and rectify their mistakes. Nor do they pay heed to good advice. But the cultured accept good advice, sincerely try to rectify their mistakes and consciously endeavour not to repeat them.

Balancing Philosophy and Emotions

Manu continued, 'My dear son, it has already been proved that you are affectionate towards your brother and are greatly aggrieved upon his death at the hands of the Yakshas. Please don't cause any further damages.'

As a child, Dhruva had been jealous of Uttama—this fact was known to many. Upon Uttama's unceremonious killing by a Yaksha, had Dhruva not taken such a step against the offenders, people would deduce that Dhruva still maintained some ill feelings towards Uttama. To prove his affection for his younger brother and the absence of any negative feelings towards him, Dhruva overreacted to Uttama's death.

> *Punishment should not be disproportionate to the crime done.*
>
> *Being affectionate to one's near and dear ones is natural and necessary but shouldn't be harmful to others.*

Sometimes, even great personalities are prone to forgetting philosophy when they encounter emotional upheavals. However, that is only circumstantial forgetfulness and does not constitute their essential nature.

Svayambhuva Manu went on. 'It is very difficult to achieve the eternal abode of Lord Hari in the Vaikuntha, but your fortune is beyond compare, for you are destined to go to Vaikuntha after leaving this world. Since you are a pure devotee of Lord Vishnu, the Lord is always thinking of you. As you are recognized by all great devotees, your life is supposed to be exemplary. I'm very surprised you have taken up the abominable task of annihilating the Yakshas.'

Dhruva was already a celebrated warrior and an accomplished devotee of Lord Vishnu. Now, the misalignment of his behaviour with his position as a devotee would bring him infamy.

To whom more is given, of them, more is expected—greater the privilege, greater the responsibility. If an illiterate person makes a mistake, the reaction may not be so fervent. But if a leader holding a responsible position commits a sin, the reaction would be intense. Also, the impact would have a wider outreach.

Svayambhuva Manu tried pacifying Dhruva with the most appropriate words. Manu expressed his surprise at Dhruva's unexpected behaviour. There is a possibility of deviating from the ideal principles right up to the last minute of reaching our goals. Continually seeking guidance from mature people, we must solidify our philosophy and principles at a rudimentary level. Also, the chief responsibility of a leader is his exemplary behaviour.

Manu suggested to Dhruva a peaceful path that was just opposite to the path of aggression and agitation.

Mature people can speak the most effective philosophy with relevance to the context. This in turn positively impacts the hearers.

Responsibility in Relationships

When one forgets one's duties, it is the duty of their well-wishers to remind them of their expected duties.

In this mood, Svayambhuva Manu informed Dhruva that he should maintain conduct that would please the Lord, not displease Him. Manu continued, 'Dear Dhruva, Lord Vishnu is completely satisfied with his devotee who deals with other people with tolerance, compassion, friendship and equality. One who satisfies the Lord by exhibiting such conduct becomes liberated from this world and attains eternal spiritual bliss. This is the power of winning the Lord's heart with one's good behaviour and conduct.'

Manu then highlighted the importance of seeing the Lord's hand in all circumstances of life. He went on, 'People enjoy and suffer the results of their own past activities. When the wind blows, particles of dust fly in the air, similarly, one suffers or enjoys according to one's particular karma.'

While the 'law of karma' teaches us to take responsibility for our pleasant and unpleasant experiences in life, immature human beings consider the cause of their suffering to be everyone but themselves. A mature spiritualist like Suniti does not blame others for her suffering but identifies oneself as the cause of her miseries. We may receive happiness or distress 'through' others but not necessarily 'from' them. Therefore, it is imprudent to blame the instrument of one's karma (as discussed in Chapter Two).

Identify the Ultimate Cause

'Lord Vishnu is the all-powerful master of everything in this world', said Manu. 'He is worshipped by great devatas, who are dependent on Him. He is the one who awards the results of one's activities. You have heard directly from Lord Vishnu that your brother Uttama was destined to die. Why then must we try rebelling against the Lord's sanction? These Yakshas are not the killers of your brother. The Lord is the cause of all causes. Your brother's birth and death were sanctioned by the Lord, and he will surely attain the destination that he deserves.'

The Lord is the neutral observer of everyone's activities and the unbiased provider of results.

What did Manu mean when he stated that Lord Vishnu is the cause of all causes? Did his statement imply that one should must refrain from taking action against the wrongdoer and accept that everything is sanctioned by the Lord? Absolutely not!

As a living entity in this world, one must be intelligent enough to avoid suffering as much as possible. But if such misery surpasses one's capacity to counteract, one has to accept the inevitable as God's will and a result of one's past deeds.

Pointing out the immediate cause of one's suffering is natural and necessary. However, identifying the ultimate cause of the misery is mandatory. For instance, the postman brings a parcel that has an attractive gift. Upon receiving the gift, you may thank the postman for bringing it to you. But the person who sent the gift to you through the courier is someone else, not the postman himself. Your ultimate gratitude for receiving the gift must be directed to your friend who lovingly sent that gift to you. Similarly, when the postman delivers a letter bearing unpleasant news, you must not hate or scold the postman for having delivered such news. The postman is just a deliverer who brings the news to you. Sometimes, the postman's arrival at your home might give you happiness and, at other times, distress. But in either case, the postman is just doing his job.

Similarly, people in this world may act in ways that might trigger trouble or happiness at times, but we shouldn't see them as the ultimate cause of our happiness or distress. They are simply instruments of our karma and in truth, all these experiences are ultimately sanctioned by the Lord.

Svayambhuva Manu began to conclude. 'My dear child, please accept the will of Lord Vishnu and stop killing the Yakshas. Turn your attention towards the Lord and regain your natural position as a devotee of the Lord without deviating from the expected consciousness and behaviour of a devotee. Give up your anger. I wish all good fortune unto you.'

Appease the Affected Party

A person who desires liberation from this world should not be enslaved by anger because uncontrollable anger is the fountainhead of downfall for one and all.

Then, Manu let Dhruva in on his last piece of advice. 'My dear Dhruva, you considered the Yakshas to be the killer of your brother, therefore, you killed them in great numbers. By this action, you have agitated the mind of the king of the Yakshas—Kuvera.

Kuvera is an intimate associate of Lord Shiva. You should immediately go and beg forgiveness from Kuvera with your gentle words and prayers. Otherwise, the wrath of such great souls may affect our family in unwanted ways.'

> *One should think and act in such a way that they become objects of compassion of the devotees, not the objects of their wrath.*

Having said this, Manu departed. Now the onus of making the right move rested on Dhruva's shoulders. Upon Manu's arrival, Dhruva had adjourned his fight with the Yakshas only to hear him speak. Would Dhruva resume fighting now? Or would he simply apologize to Kuvera, the king of Yakshas? How would Kuvera react to Dhruva's actions? Would he forgive or admonish him? Flip the page to find out.

* * *

Pearls of Wisdom

Relationship Sutras

1. Dismissing a wise man's opinion is like dismissing the visible path to perfection.
2. Punishing others should bring out the best in them, not the worst of our rage.
3. Punishment can be served through arrows that wound or injections that heal.
4. Circumstantial outbursts are common, but diligence will bring about restraint.
5. Speaking context-friendly philosophy positively impacts others.
6. Extend yourself to help others when they go astray.
7. Don't think and act in a way that agitates others.
8. Be dutiful and remind others of their duty when they forget.
9. While selfish agendas expressed through violence are barbaric, selfless service accompanied by necessary violence brings about true peace.

Success Sutras

1. Humbly invite constructive feedback and corrections.
2. Give your elders the opportunity to correct you.
3. Don't be stubborn and highly opinionated.
4. Cultivate the right discrimination to use violence.
5. Don't condemn others out of love for your dear ones.
6. Uphold the expectations of your position.
7. The answer to the question of whether we need guidance is in the question itself.
8. A surgeon and a thief use knives. Are both violent?
9. Responsibility is your ability to respond. Treat them not as heavy burdens but as chances to get out the best that's rotting within you.

15

Conflict Resolution in Mature Circles

A mistake is a mistake if one fails to learn from it. Honest regret, sincere apology, the effort to improve and endeavour not to repeat—bring one to the platform of perfection.

Dhruva was impressed. The good counsel given by his grandfather Svayambhuva Manu had a penetrating effect on his mind. His anger subsided and his fierce countenance had been restored to that of a sober, composed and mature emperor. He realized that he had been victimized by unbridled anger. Thus, he immediately restrained himself from further bloodshed. He admitted that he had killed several Yakshas unnecessarily and thus displeased the king of Yakshas, Kuvera—a great soul. He prepared himself to meet Kuvera and apologize for his outrageous behaviour.

Genuine repentance for one's mistakes impels one to better oneself and sincerely endeavour to avoid them in the future.

Kuvera was the blessed master of the heavenly treasury and the king of the Yaksha race too. He got to know of Dhruva's anger which had now caved in. He also heard how Dhruva had discontinued the decimation of the Yakshas. No sooner did Kuvera receive this news than he appeared before Dhruva. The Yakshas, Kinnaras, Charanas and many other celestial beings accompanied him.

Maturity in Conflict Resolution

Dhruva folded his hands and bowed down to Kuvera in respect. Then Kuvera spoke to Dhruva, 'O sinless kshatriya, I am gladdened to know that you have given up your strife with the Yakshas upon being advised by your grandfather Manu. I am very pleased with you.'

Dhruva realized his mistake and was apologetic to Kuvera while Kuvera acknowledged Dhruva's regret and forgave him. An egoistic person doesn't acknowledge his mistakes and apologize for them, instead, he remains unbending in terms of his attitude and actions. But Dhruva wasn't attached to his ego. Those who are too egoistic cannot forgive people even when they sincerely apologize for their mistakes. They continue to maintain grudges and hatred towards those who have committed the mistake. Interestingly, Kuvera wasn't like that. Since Dhruva and Kuvera were mature and wise, the conflict between them was easily resolved.

Mistakes are made—sometimes small, sometimes big. Depending on the gravity of the situation, one may take corrective action against the wrongdoer. Bearing long-term grudges only toxifies relationships.

Kuvera addressed Dhruva as sinless. How does this make sense? In truth, Dhruva considered himself sinful for having killed numerous Yakshas, but Kuvera wanted to assure Dhruva that, in essence, he had not killed the Yakshas. How was it so? Kuvera clarified, 'Dear Dhruva, you have not killed the Yakshas, nor have they killed your brother! This is because the ultimate cause of birth and death is the eternal time factor, a feature of the Supreme Lord. One who is destined to die at some point in life will undoubtedly encounter death no matter what. All of one's attempts towards self-preservation cannot help one escape death. Even if you haven't killed the Yakshas, still being subservient to the laws of nature, they were bound to perish. However, the soul can never be killed. It is only the body which is killed by an agent when the appropriate time comes.'

Time causes all transformations in this world and is neutral to everyone. It bears no alliance or animosity towards anyone.

It is by the Lord's arrangement that one receives the results of one's past activities in the form of happiness or distress via the channel of different agents.

An Unexpected Boon

Dhruva silently heard as Kuvera spoke. Dhruva's respectfulness and obedience shaped his behaviour. Kuvera went on. 'My dear Dhruva, may the Lord always grace you with good fortune. He is the ultimate shelter of all living beings. Please engage yourself in worshipping and serving Him as you are already accustomed. We have heard about your exalted devotion. I am very pleased with your submissiveness to elders. I wish to offer you a boon. Please ask whatever you want from me.'

Being thus requested by Kuvera, Dhruva replied thus—'Dear Sir, may I have unflinching faith unto Lord Vishnu and may I constantly remember him and thus cross over this ocean of nescience with ease and grace.'

Knowing well that Kuvera was the treasurer of the devatas and the wealthiest person in the world, Dhruva could have asked him for a bountiful supply of wealth. But Dhruva had desired not wealth nor any position in this world. He had severed the strings of attachment to temporary positions and possessions right from his childhood. This was because he had found real value in life—devotion to the Lord.

Can a fish brought out of the water be satisfied by any amount of money, fame, followers, facilities, comforts, and so on? All we need to do to make the fish happy is put it back in the water. Similarly, a living being, which is by nature spiritual, cannot survive in the material ambiance, however attractive it may be. This is because it hankers for permanent pleasure in the spiritual atmosphere. Although this is the case with most people in the world, not many realize what satisfies them!

> *One who realizes one's incompatibility with the material world and simultaneously identifies with one's true spiritual nature lives a spiritually-oriented life. Discharging one's duties in this world, along with such an orientation leads one to eternal success.*

Material possessions stay with us for some time during our life and leave us after a while. Even if they do stay to the point we draw our last breath, we leave them when we turn up our toes. We can't take with us even a single penny, what then to speak of storehouses full of millions? Having understood this well, mature people gather only so much wealth as is required for sustenance. They do not chase riches out of greed. Rather, they focus on things that are permanent in nature. Such permanence is only found in devotion unto the Lord, which yields eternal returns of unfading spiritual bliss.

Everyone endeavours for peace, happiness and satisfaction. But the joys of this material world are fleeting. Therefore, wise people, instead of pursuing the impermanent pleasures of this world, aspire for an eternal life of loving service unto the Lord. This is possible only in the spiritual realm. To enjoy eternal bliss in the company of the Lord is the very nucleus of the soul. The spirit soul cannot be satisfied by the increase of wealth, name, fame, position and other material possessions that are lost one day.

> *Wealth, position and possessions in this world are not worth hankering for, for they are temporary and are destined to leave us some day or the other.*
>
> *One whose heart is rich with devotion to the Lord doesn't aspire for any riches of this world.*

Dhruva's heart has already tasted the joy of devotion. Why would he ask Kuvera for any material wealth? Although he was circumstantially overwhelmed with anger due to his brother's death, his position as an exalted devotee was intact. One mistake committed by a devotee does not degrade his position as a devotee.

Blessings are beyond the Giver

Another question! Dhruva's position as a devotee of Lord Vishnu is higher than the position of Kuvera. Then how could Kuvera bless Dhruva with unflinching devotion? Narada Muni and Suniti were more exalted devotees when they blessed and inspired Dhruva to worship the Lord. But now Dhruva was already a successful devotee who was destined to go to Vaikuntha. So how could Kuvera bless Dhruva?

Although Dhruva had a deep devotion for the Lord, he still begged for devotion from Kuvera because, in the first place, he had no interest in any riches that Kuvera might bestow upon him. Secondly, he was concerned that the displeasure of Kuvera might obstruct his personal remembrance of the Lord.

> *The displeasure of great souls obstructs our meditation and remembrance of the Lord.*

Therefore, one should not cause trouble to anyone in this world unnecessarily, whether they are devotees or not, human beings or animals, men or women, children or elders, brahmanas or kshatriyas. Whatever may be the caste, creed, gender, nationality and species of the other living being, a wise person never disrespects anyone. A noble-hearted person is naturally inclined to have loving and friendly dealings with everyone. One may have only a few close friends and may not have very close relationships with everyone, still, one should be polite, respectful and cordial with whomever one meets in this world. Because when one hurts or displeases another person unnecessarily, their displeasure acts as an obstacle to one's devotion.

Kuvera was immensely pleased to bestow the boon that Dhruva asked for. Thereafter, Kuvera disappeared while Dhruva returned to his kingdom and performed his royal responsibilities as usual. He conducted several sacrifices to please Lord Vasudeva. He gave a profuse amount of charity to the people who attended his sacrifices. He always meditated on the Lord and protected his citizens like a loving father.

Exceptional Rule and Exemplary Retirement

Dhruva was endowed with all good qualities. He was respectful to elders, kind to the poor and an upholder of dharma. With all these qualities, he ruled his citizens considering himself as their servant, and not a controller.

> *The mood of controllership and dictatorship rule the minds of malicious rulers, but virtuous rulers are those who rule with responsibility and retire with detachment.*

Dhruva thus ruled the kingdom for 36,000 years and then planned for his retirement. Finally, he left his kingdom, family, treasury, comfortable palaces, army, friends, followers and so on and retired to the forest in the Himalayas. He went to a holy place known as 'Badarikashram', inhabited by several sages and spiritual seekers.

Dhruva's life at Badarikashram was exemplary. As a renounced saint, he constantly worshipped and meditated on Lord Vishnu in the company of sages. In devotional ecstasy, he used to shed incessant tears of love for the Lord. His heart melted, his body shivered and his hair stood on end as he entered into a deep trance while meditating on the Lord.

How did Dhruva reach Dhruvaloka? The next (and last) chapter reveals the exciting details.

* * *

Pearls of Wisdom

Relationships

1. Repentance doesn't connote endless remorse. The quality of your repentance is visible in the future course of your action.
2. Holding grudges is letting a despised person occupy a rent-free land in your little head.
3. Great souls are those stable bridges who connect us to God. Can we crossover if we cause cracks on those bridges? Be respectful earlier to prevent regret later.

Success Sutras

1. While controlling time is inexorable, utilizing it is optional.
2. Understand your true spiritual nature, and do the needful in the material world.
3. Curtail the mood of controllership and dictatorship.
4. Govern with responsibility and retire with detachment.
5. For the soul this world is foreign. Be a holiday maker, not a stress receptor.
6. Don't decorate the golden cage (body) forever. Remember to nourish the hungry bird (soul) that's starving within.

7. A leader doesn't aspire to dictate to others but desires to dictate himself for the welfare of others.
8. Perform your work passionately while repeatedly pressing on the purpose you were working for.

16

Unfading Gratitude

Life's two greatest tests are—1. Consistency amidst failures and 2. Humility amidst success. One who passes them is a truly successful person.

One day, at Badarikashram, as Dhruva was engaged in his spiritual practices as usual, he saw an effulgent airplane coming towards him. The divine airplane was shining resplendently, illuminating all directions—it was as brilliant as the moon. It was driven by two beautiful personalities whose forms resembled Lord Vishnu. They were the *Vishnudutas* or the messengers of Lord Vishnu, named Nanda and Sunanda.

The Vaikuntha Men in the Airplane

Nanda and Sunanda were youthful—they had four hands, an ebony bodily lustre and their eyes resembled reddish lotus flowers. They were dressed in attractive garments and wore excellent crowns, necklaces, bracelets and earrings. Seeing these uncommon personalities who were the direct servants of Lord Vishnu in Vaikuntha, Dhruva immediately stood up in respect. He was elated and puzzled. In great haste, he forgot to receive them properly. But he simply bowed down to them, stood with folded hands and started chanting the names of the Lord, 'Jai Narayana! Jai Gopal! Jai Govinda!' Dhruva was always absorbed in thinking of Lord Vishnu. His heart was filled with love for Lord Vasudeva.

Nanda and Sunanda spoke to Dhruva, who stood amidst an assembly of great sages. They said, 'Dear Dhruva, let there be good fortune unto you. When you were five years old, you underwent severe austerities, thereby greatly satisfying Lord Vishnu. We are His representatives and servants known as the Vishnudutas. He has deputed us to bring you to His eternal abode Vaikuntha now. To attain Vishnuloka or Vaikuntha is extremely rare, but you have attained this good fortune by your sincere austerities and devotion. Neither your forefathers nor anyone else before you ever attained Vaikuntha. The sun, the moon, the stars and all the other planets, lunar mansions, and solar systems are circumambulating Lord Vishnu's abode, where Lord Vishnu personally resides, being lovingly worshipped and served by its inhabitants. Please come with us and live there eternally. That divine planet will be known as Dhruvaloka henceforth. You're welcome. O immortal one, this unique airplane has been sent by the Lord, who is worshipped by select prayers. You're quite worthy to board such an airplane.'

> *No mechanical process can take one to Vaikuntha—it is only by sincere devotion or bhakti yoga one can attain Vaikuntha.*

Dhruva was immensely dear to Lord Vishnu. Being successful in pleasing the Lord, he made his mother, father, teacher and even the Lord proud of him. This was his life's success. Everyone admired his determination in austerity, devotion to the Lord and diligence in his rule. Now that glorious Dhruva was attaining his final destination in the Dhruvaloka, which was none other than Lord Vishnu's abode.

Being Grounded in Success

Upon being lovingly invited by the Vishnudutas into the Vaikuntha airplane, Dhruva bowed down to them. He then took a sacred bath, dressed in suitable clothing and performed his daily worship. Then he bowed down to all the sages at Badarikashram and received their blessings. Thereafter, he prepared himself to board the airplane.

Although Dhruva was just about to ascend to the Vaikuntha in the airplane that had been personally sent by Lord Vishnu, still, he did not give up his daily 'worship'. In fact, worship or service of the Lord is not done just to attain a particular goal. The real goal of life is to serve the Lord constantly. In the process of bhakti, the 'goal' and the 'means' of attaining the goal are the same. We worship and serve the Lord to be able to serve Him eternally and perfectly. In the practice stage, there may be some flaws in our service, but in the stage of perfection, one is constantly absorbed in the bliss of service to the Lord.

> *The eternal activity of every soul is to serve the Lord. Absorption in such a loving service is the identity of every living being.*

Humility in Success and Consistency in Failures

Another important aspect of learning from Dhruva's character is that he did not give up his 'respect' for the sages at Badarikashram. The Vaikuntha airplane came to take Dhruva to Vaikuntha and not the sages. In that sense, Dhruva was more qualified than the sages wherein he was eligible to enter Vaikuntha, while many brahmana sages present there were not.

Of course, sometimes those who are eligible to stay in Vaikuntha may stay in this world by the Lord's will, just to guide other people in their spiritual lives. But the humility exhibited by Dhruva is noteworthy here. He was bowing down and seeking the blessings of several people just before entering Vaikuntha. Why would he need anyone's blessings now and to accomplish what? He had already attained the pinnacle of success—an entrance into Vaikuntha. But he had no tinge of pride. He did not become puffed up because the airplane had been sent by Vishnu to take him to Vaikuntha and not the sages there. He was genuinely humble in seeking the blessings of the sages before riding on the plane.

> *The greatest success of a person is not just in accomplishing goals but also in maintaining a humble demeanour even after achieving the goal.*

We are tested for two things in life. Firstly, we are tested for our consistency in failures. Secondly, we are tested for our humility in success. One who faces failures in life might lose inspiration to consistently continue one's efforts and one who is successful might become proud or puffed up of one's accomplishments. But those who have devotion to the Lord are neither inconsistent in failures nor proud in successes. They remain consistent in their attempts despite facing failures. They don't feel discouraged, disappointed, demotivated or disheartened. By demonstrating great consistency in one's attempts, many people in universal history have attained success in their goals. At the same time, despite being successful in attaining the most difficult to attain goals in life, they remained humble and grounded. These are the 'real ingredients for success'.

> *Failures are common, but one shouldn't become inconsistent in one's attempts. Success is great, but one shouldn't become puffed up or intoxicated.*

Offered with Grace, Not Demanded with Arrogance

Before boarding the Vaikuntha airplane, Dhruva worshipped and circumambulated the airplane with devotion. Thereafter, he offered his respects to the Vishnudutas who brought the airplane in front of him. Just as Lord Vishnu is worshippable, similarly, his associates, paraphernalia, airplane and abode are also worshippable and spiritual. The Vaikuntha airplane, which appeared in front of Dhruva was not an ordinary material airplane made of some metals—it was a spiritual airplane that moves at the will of the Lord and his devotees. Anything spiritual has no birth or death and is eternal. Dhruva understood the greatness of the Vaikuntha airplane. Therefore, he worshipped the airplane before boarding it.

Dhruva did not take the airplane and the opportunity to enter Vaikuntha for granted. He accepted this privilege with great respect and gratitude. Such an opportunity is offered with grace but not demanded with arrogance. While a humble person accepts it with gratitude, an arrogant person thinks of oneself as entitled to it and demands it.

We shouldn't take success for granted for it is by the support and blessings of so many people that we have achieved it.

When the attitude of gratitude overpowers the mood of entitlement, one values the privileges received—otherwise, one demands for rights and becomes puffed up.

Success of Attaining Deathlessness

Dhruva didn't die as an ordinary human. An average human being may leave the body in some accident due to being afflicted by a disease or being killed by someone. Dhruva's soul did not leave the body like that. Dhruva boarded the airplane not caring for death. He placed his foot on the head of death personified and boarded the airplane in an effulgent spiritual body. He became as brilliant and as illuminating as molten gold.

Dhruva's body became spiritual. In this spiritual body, Dhruva would be entering Vaikuntha to remain as an eternal associate of Lord Vishnu for eternity. There is no birth, disease, old age or death on the spiritual planet of Vaikuntha, where nothing is subjected to deterioration or destruction.

Dhruva wasn't afraid of death personified. Death troubles everyone but not the Lord's devotees. A cat carries kittens in her mouth and also carries rats in her mouth. However, both these cases are not similar. For a kitten, the cat acts like a loving mother. But for the rats, the cat is death personified. Similarly, death threatens every living being with fear whereas death causes no fear in the heart of a devotee of Vishnu or Krishna.

For devotees, death is not leaving home and relatives but reaching the real home and relatives.

In this world, we connect with others through temporary bodies. Bodily relationships and the resultant pleasure are temporary. But if we connect with someone on a spiritual plane by identifying oneself and others as children of God, that is a spiritual relationship that is everlasting and eternal. All of us are connected with each other, with God in the centre as our supreme, loving father.

Celebrating Others' Success

When Dhruva was boarding the airplane, drums and kettledrums resounded in the sky. Celestial beings like *Gandharvas* and *Apsaras* began to sing and dance, and various devatas showered flowers like torrents of rain upon Dhruva. All the sages at Badarikashram were happy to bid farewell to Dhruva, who had attained the unparalleled spiritual success of attaining Vaikuntha. No one was envious of Dhruva and everyone wholeheartedly celebrated his success. Because Dhruva himself wasn't envious of anyone there, he didn't attract anyone's envy.

> *In cultured societies, where appreciation for each other is prevalent, envy finds no place to reside.*
>
> *Envy is, in essence, indirect appreciation. Instead of envying those better than us, if only we begin appreciating their merit, we can have enlivening relationships.*

Thus, Dhruva sat in the Vaikuntha airplane driven by Lord Vishnu's personal associates, Nanda and Sunanda. The plane was about to take off through outer space to reach Vishnuloka.

An Unexpected Thought!

'No, I cannot go to Vaikuntha!' Dhruva thought. Something bothered his mind seriously. At this momentous moment of ascending to Vaikuntha to meet the Lord, Dhruva thought, 'Let me jump off this airplane.' He could not move ahead. As the airplane was moving, Dhruva became very anxious.

'How can I go alone to Vaikuntha without my mother?' He questioned himself within his mind. Was he being sentimental? Was that a material attachment to bodily relationships? The relationships with mother, father, brother, sister, wife, children and so on are all based on a person's presence within a body! When a person leaves the body, all these relationships are ended. And the person who dies enters another body according to one's moods and deeds. Dhruva, being a spiritually elevated personality, attained a spiritual body at the end of his long life of 36,000 years and was now going to Vaikuntha. Being so spiritually advanced, was him remembering his mother who gave birth to his body and getting overwhelmed with emotions justified?

The answer is a big 'Yes'. What appeared in Dhruva's mind at this moment was the feeling of 'gratitude', which was spiritual. Even on a material plane, the quality of 'gratitude' is worth appreciating.

Gratitude is the foundational virtue of human relationships! Of all disgraceful behaviour, there is nothing worse than ingratitude.

Dhruva was deeply grateful to his virtuous mother, Suniti. He thought, 'It is my mother who has inspired me to worship Lord Vishnu and it was only by her guidance, inspiration and blessings that I am attaining this fortune of entering Vaikuntha.'

Spiritualizing Relationships

Although we may connect and interact with people through material bodies, our relationships need not be material. We can spiritualize our relationships by bringing God into the centre. Mother Suniti certainly had given birth to Dhruva and thus in one sense, their relationship was based on the body. But that bodily relationship was converted into a spiritual relationship when Suniti gave Dhruva spiritual inspiration and acted as a spiritual teacher by guiding him to worship Lord Vishnu. Through her initial inspiration and guidance, Dhruva eventually became very advanced in spiritual life, which is why he could now enter Vaikuntha. At this moment of success of human life, Dhruva did not forget the favour shown by his mother. His heart became overwhelmed with gratitude.

> *While qualities like anger, lust, envy, pride and greed are unfavourable to one's progressive life, qualities like compassion, gratitude and humility are essential for a fulfilling life.*

Dhruva is able to go to the spiritual world because he has all the devotional qualities like compassion, gratitude and so on.

Suniti acted like a '*pathapradarshaka* guru' or the teacher who showed him the way to reach God. Sometimes, a pathapradarshaka guru can also be called a *shiksha* guru or a teacher who instructs us how to perform service to the Lord. Narada Muni was certainly the *diksha* guru, the spiritual master who initiated Dhruva into chanting the mantra 'om namo bhagavata vasudevaya' and taught him in detail the process of worship and meditation. Narada Muni was a pure devotee and *sannyasi* who is engaged in the great service of teaching bhakti to everyone. Dhruva was certainly grateful to Narada Muni, but he didn't become anxious that he was leaving behind Narada Muni and going to Vaikuntha. He knew well enough that Narada Muni could go to Vaikuntha whenever he wanted and have a direct conversation with Lord Vishnu. But Dhruva worried about his mother Suniti and wanted her also to go to Vaikuntha with him. This was not out of bodily attachment but spiritual gratitude since the mother and son shared a divine spiritual relationship with the Lord in the centre.

God's Duty Is to Fulfil Devotee's Desires

The Lord is always eager to fulfil the desires of His devotees and the devotee is also completely dependent on the Lord's sanction and decision—that's how they share their sacred relationship. Here, Dhruva desired to take his mother to Vaikuntha and how can the Lord not fulfil that wish? The Lord had fulfilled all the wishes of Dhruva when he was a five-year-old. Now when he was more than 36,000 years old, but the Lord's desire to fulfil

His devotee's desire didn't slacken. And of course, Suniti herself was a great devotee of Lord Vishnu, the one who inspired devotion in Dhruva. So, why would the Lord have any reservations about taking her to Vaikuntha?

Even before a devotee wishes something, the Lord is prepared to fulfil all those wishes.

As Dhruva was thinking of jumping off the Vaikuntha airplane, Nanda and Sunanda, who understood his mind, showed him something exciting that made Dhruva blissful. They said, 'Dear Dhruva, see you there.' They pointed to another effulgent Vaikuntha airplane that was going in the sky, carrying mother Suniti. Dhruva's happiness knew no bounds. His heart was completely satisfied to see his mother on the way to Vaikuntha along with him.

This is the power of bhakti. Even a disciple can take one's guru to the spiritual world through the power of one's bhakti. Of course, in this case, Suniti herself was a wonderful devotee of Lord Vishnu. However, Dhruva's austerities, tapasya and the intensity of his bhakti were unparalleled. Although Suniti could not go to the forest or perform such severe austerities as Dhruva did, she was still going to Vaikuntha by virtue of guiding a glorious son like Dhruva.

Even if one is unable to render a specific service to the Lord, if one inspires and guides others in that service, one gets benefitted.

On the Way to Pole Star

While Dhruva was passing through outer space, he could see all the planets of the solar system and the devatas. The devatas were traveling in their airplanes showering flowers upon him like rain. Passing through Bhur, Bhuvar and Svarga-lokas, Dhruva's airplane finally reached Dhruvaloka, the self-effulgent Pole Star that illuminates all other planets and is circumambulated by all the luminaries. It was none other than the personal abode of Lord Vishnu, the ultimate destination of all spiritual seekers and devotees. Dhruvaloka is higher than even the 'saptarishi mandala', the planets of the seven great sages.

Only those people who are constantly serving the Lord in the welfare activities of common living beings can attain Vaikuntha. Ordinary material heaven can be attained by performing a few pious activities. However, the spiritual abode of Vaikuntha can be attained only by selfless devotion to the Lord and compassion for all living beings. Persons who are peaceful, equipoised, purified, know the art of pleasing all living beings and are inclined to keep spiritual friendships and relationships with everyone, can attain the perfection of reaching Vaikuntha.

Celebrating the Success

The wonderful story of Dhruva teaches us great lessons on determination, relationships and the process of attaining success. This unimaginable historical success of Dhruva should inspire devotion and determination in us and teach us the path of attaining success most effectively while cultivating heart-warming relationships.

Dhruva's determination to attain his goals is a great example for all people to follow. His exemplary resolve inspired and shall continue to inspire millions of people on this planet. His story is worth recollecting, discussing and reflecting upon.

Even the guru of Dhruva, Narada Muni, praised Dhruva's greatly adventurous activities as he spoke to many others in the universe. Just as a father is very happy to see his son's advancement in every respect, similarly, a guru becomes happy to observe the ascendancy of one's disciple. This is the quality of a glorious master. Ordinary material masters want to oppress or suppress their subordinates and dependents, and exercise their superiority or dominion over them. On the contrary, spiritual masters or gurus are those who sincerely celebrate the success of their dependents without pride but with appreciation. So, let us become successful in our spiritual lives and social lives by taking tips for success and relationships from Dhruva's story and also learning the art of celebrating others' success.

The Supreme Lord is unconquerable. No one can conquer him. But the Lord becomes conquered by the devotion of His devotees, so much so that he happily gives himself and his personal abode to his devotees. To that degree, the Lord can be captivated by a loving devotion. Dhruva attained this exalted position at the age of five and attained Vaikuntha within just one life without wasting many. Hearing such glorious stories of great souls is a wonderful way of learning life lessons for a successful life.

* * *

Pearls of Wisdom

Relationship Sutras

1. Realize your identity as a child of God and cultivate love for Him.
2. Cultivate appreciation, not envy.
3. Never be ungrateful.
4. Nourish the seeds of compassion, gratitude and humility.

Success Sutras

1. Be humble and grounded even after accomplishing the goal.
2. Let failures not dwindle your consistency.
3. Let success not fan your pride.
4. Be grateful to those who supported and blessed you on your way to success.
5. Don't take success for granted.
6. Let your gratitude overpower the mood of entitlement.
7. Value the privileges received instead of demanding for rights.
8. Intentions are the soul of our actions.
9. Let failures inspire you to reject remorse and re-use the lessons learnt.

10. Enjoy your slice of success while recognizing the ingredients that made it palatable.
11. Death isn't an alarm to induce fear, it's a reminder to scrutinize things worthier.
12. Gratitude is equal to gratefulness minus the attitude.
13. When God takes centre stage in one's relationships, satisfaction is deepened and strains are destroyed.
14. The taller the tree, the deeper are its roots. Ground yourself deeply to soar up highly.

Acknowledgements

Words fall short of expressing my gratitude to Srila Prabhupada, the founder Acharya of the International Society for Krishna Consciousness, who presented the magnum opus Srimad Bhagavatam with his lucid explanations. It is through the lens of his illuminating purports that I have learnt to understand the depth of the Bhagavatam stories and characters.

I am forever indebted to my beloved guru, His Holiness Radhanath Swami, the founder of Govardhan Ecovillage and an international bestselling author, for enlightening me on the ideal mood of scriptural study and encouraging me with his kind blessings. I express my earnest gratitude to Gauranga Prabhu, my mentor and source of inspiration in my spiritual life.

I can't thank Parth Shah enough for his patient editing of the manuscript with precision and enthusiasm. My heartfelt gratitude to Preeti Choudhary for her dedicated efforts in being a wonderful scribe. With the honest and selfless efforts of these two persons, the book took such a beautiful shape. I sincerely thank Tanay for his wonderful inputs and Mother Radhika Kasturi for proofreading the book.

My heartfelt thanks to Gurveen, Aparna and Radhika from the Penguin team for their wonderful support and coordination in publishing this book. Finally, I heartily thank all the wonderful readers of my books.